Hudson Valley & Vicinity Attractions

New York City's Play

Copyright May 201

ISBN 978168637892

G000138683

William (Bill) C. McE

Preface

This tourist guide is based on data researched from the Internet. The author lived for many years in the Hudson Valley and has visited many of the locations, but not all and thus is depending on the accuracy of the Internet to fill in the blanks.

The name and address of each site, the GPS of each, and where possible photos of each are included in this comprehensive guide to the Hudson Valley from above New York City (NYC) to Albany (State Capital). The guide covers several counties, and there is an Appendix listing of each county and the cities within; this will make it easier to plan a trip as one can visit all the sites in a county and then cross each off his or her *'To do List'*. Additionally, for those that love wine, there is a listing of the Hudson Valley orchards, vineyards, and wineries.

Here is a sample of the Index...

D & H Canal Park 9
Depuy Canal House 9
Deyo Hall 9
Dia:Beacon 10
Discovery of Cement Marker 10
   Brooklyn Bridge and the Statue of Liberty 10
Eleanor Roosevelt Center-Val-Kill 10
Furgary Fishing Village 11
   Shacks', the 'Shantytown', 'North Dock Tin Boat Association' 11
Glynwood (Org) Farm 11
   Regenerative Agriculture 12
Gomez Mill House 12
Harden House 13
   Union Free School District of Tarrytown 13
   Old Croton Aqueduct Trail 13
Hudson River Sloop Clearwater 13

Table of Contents

Hudson Valley & Vicinity Attractions..1
  Preface 1
  Table of Contents...2
  Chapter # 01 ... Attractions 3
  Chapter # 02 ... Beaches 35
  Chapter # 03 ... Bridges...37
  Chapter # 04 ... Campgrounds...39
  Chapter # 05 ... Climbing Areas 45
  Chapter # 06 ... Graves & Burial Plots 47
  Chapter # 07 ... Hiking Trails..49
  Chapter # 08 ... Historic Buildings/ Sites & Markers 62
  Chapter # 09 ... Historical Societies...72
  Chapter # 10 ... Lighthouses..73
  Chapter # 11 ... Military History Sites 75
  Chapter # 12 ... Museums..81
  Chapter # 13 ... Parks 96
  Chapter # 14 ... Railroads & Rail Trails 99
  Chapter # 15 ... RV Campgrounds 104
  Chapter # 16 ... Skiing Areas...106
  Chapter # 17 ... Tours/Fairs & Fun Things to Do.......................108
  Chapter # 18 ... Wineries 111
  Chapter # 19 ... Waterfalls 116
  Chapter # 20 ... Zoos & Animal Parks 119
  Appendix I - County City/Town Listing.....................................120
  Index 123
  Author 135
  Cover Picture...136

Using this Touring Manual:

The reader is advised to use mapping programs such as Google Maps™ to verify the locations provided, and to map out his or her course of travel each day. Readers can also find places to eat, stay, fuel up, etc., from most of the mapping programs.

This guide does NOT contain that type of information and has received NO stipends or other compensation from the establishments in this touring manual.

Chapter # 01 ... Attractions

This chapter has dozens of interesting attractions within the confines of the Hudson River Valley from New York City to Albany, and from the edge of the Catskill Mountains to the border with Connecticut. These items of interest are those that do not fall into the categories of Museums, Waterfalls, Hiking trails, camping grounds, or rides, etc, which are described or shown in the remaining chapters of this Hudson Valley touring and Attractions Guide. All items are *listed alphabetically*, many have a short description, and all have the physical and Geographical addresses. Restaurants (Unless in an historic building), motels, hotels, phone numbers and websites have NOT been includes as these attributes can and often do change.

5 Locks Walk

Delaware and Hudson Canal from Locks 16 to 20

D&H Canal Historical Society

Rosendale Hydraulic Cement

These canal locks have been preserved by the *D&H Canal Historical Society* and are part of the history of the area in that back when the canal was first constructed it brought '*Anthracite Coal*' and lumber to the NYC area; while digging the 108 mile long canal they discovered '*Rosendale Hydraulic Cement*' that allowed for the construction of many of the iconic buildings of NYC as well as the *Brooklyn Bridge* and the *Statue of Lib*erty.

The 1825 canal lasted from 1828 and 1899, but was replaced by railroads and other means of transport. Today there are sections still in existence in Pennsylvania and New York, and several towns were named for the developers. There are museums along the route that display how the gravity railroads and canal locks worked. Plan on two or more hours.

5 Locks Walk
1 2nd Street,
High Falls, NY 12440
41.827058, -74.127446

Albert K. Smiley Memorial Tower (Skytop Tower)

The Alvert K. Smiley Memorial Tower. Erected in grateful memory of a man whose exalted character and useful life stand as a beautiful example to mankind. Born March 17, 1828. Died December 2, 1912. The corner stone was laid August 30, 1921

This is a hike for many and is a once in a lifetime adventure. The tower stands on top of the mountain and overlooks the *Mohonk Mountain House & Resort* and a major part of the Hudson Valley at New Paltz, New York. The view overlooks a small kidney shaped lake.

{Picture is a snippet from the outdoorproject.com website}

There are two paths to the tower, one that is sloping and reasonably gentle on the body, and the second that is rocky, has ladders, and goes through a deep crevice that some nicknamed as the *Lemon Squeeze*.

If you have claustrophobia, then do NOT take the Labyrinth climb; use the sloping paths. The path is frequently used in the winter for skiing.

Note. If you park at the visitor's center the walk to the tower is very long, many will go to the resort and pay the $20 plus fee that will allow for a less lengthily walk. If staying at the resort the fee may be waved. Plan on spending from three to four hours.

Skytop Tower,
High Falls, NY 12440
GPS 41.763583, -74.156009

Boscobel House and Gardens

From the boscobel.org website.

> *"Built between 1804 and 1808, Boscobel was originally the dream house of wealthy Loyalists. By the 1950s, after falling into disrepair, it was demolished. Preservationists saved as many architectural fragments as possible and reassembled them fifteen miles north, where the Neoclassical mansion was restored back to – and even beyond – its original grandeur."*

Reader's Digest co-founder *Lila Acheson Wallace* raised the funds to buy the leftover pieces of the original building in 1955. The building had been sold to a wrecking firm for $35 and demolished; Wallace managed to have it restored to its neoclassical mansion look as it is appears today.

{Photo from the paththroughhistory.iloveny.com website}

The building houses displays are mostly from the 1790's - 1820's period and feature New York furniture and many decorative artwork items. The furniture includes chairs, tables, dressers, and much more.

The grounds face the Hudson River and the U.S. West Point Military Academy's Constitution Marsh area and thus, present great views and even better photos.

Open days and hours are on their website, and it is advisable that you consult it for information on tours and fees, including free visit times and dates, and holiday closings. Plan on one to two hours.

Boscobel House and Gardens,
1601 NY-9D,
Garrison, NY 10524
GPS 41.411770, -73.939256

Carrollcliff

Axe Castle

Equus Restaurant

General Howard Carroll built this Tudor style castle from local stone while he worked for the New York Times as a political and traveling correspondent. In 1940 the property became a boy's school. Axe Houghton Securities then renamed it to *Axe Castle*, but later it was renamed the *Equus* and is now a restaurant. Plan on 30 minutes to look around at the beauty of the castle and architecture, much longer if eating there.

Equus
400 Benedict Ave,
Tarrytown, NY 10591
41.067071, -73.848752

Catskill Mountains

Borscht Belt

Shawangunk Mountains

The *Catskill Mountains* for decades was known for being the playground of the folks from NYC, especially those of Jewish decent. The area was accessed by NY Route # 52 the went through Newburg, Pine Bush, and Ellenville to what was known as the *'Borscht Belt'* a conglomeration of resorts like *Grossinger's Catskill Resort Hotel, Brown's Hotel,* the *Nevele Resort,* and such. There is also the Monticello Raceway a famous horseracing track.

Over the years Route # 17, (Soon to be an Interstate I-86) was improved and became the main road to the Catskills and this bypassed Route # 52, and thus nearly and in some instances totally destroying the resorts and the area's prime income sources. Today the Catskills are being reopened by *Native American Casino Resorts* and by those folks that do not mind the 80+-mile drive to work in the city each day.

The Catskills are part of the Hudson Valley as you get above Kingston. The mountains are NOT part of the Hudson Valley below the Kingston area as there is another mountain range between the

Hudson River and the Catskill Range, that being the *Shawangunk Mountains* a continuation of the *Pocono Mountains* of Pennsylvania. The Shawangunk Mountains afford excellent hiking, climbing, swimming, and great views of the Hudson Valley around the New Paltz area.

Catskills Visitor Center

This is a good place to get maps, trail info, etc. about the Catskills in the upper Hudson Valley area.

Catskills Visitor Center
5096 NY-28,
Mt Tremper, NY 12457
42.028002, -74.269760

Cedar Grove

See the Thomas Cole's Cedar Grove write-up

Colden Mansion Ruins

Closed on Saturdays and Sundays

> *Site of Colden Mansion built of stone in 1767 by Cadwallader Colden Jr. Estate established in 1727 area since, Coldenham. Walden Woman's Club.*

There is a dispute over the cemetery that may contain the remains of folk from the Revolutionary War era, and beyond. There are plans to make the entire estate into a local park. The Colden family has a history of government and scientific service and their name is part of the history of the Hudson Valley and some of its towns. Plan on 30 minutes.

Colden Mansion Ruins,
455 NY-17K,
Rock Tavern, NY 12575
GPS 41.526570, -74.133148

Constitution Marsh Audubon Center and Sanctuary

This 270-acre tidal wetland is home to some 200-bird species, and some 30 fish species as well as to many other animal and reptile species. There is a boardwalk that allows you to venture out into the marshland and view nature at its finest. Plan on two to three hours.

Constitution Marsh Audubon Center and Sanctuary
127 Warren Landing Road,
Garrison, NY 10524
41.402158, -73.938475

Boardwalk Area

Cold Spring, NY 10516
41.402395, -73.939929

Parking Area

113 Indian Brook Road
Garrison, NY 10524
41.404238, -73.934069

Decker House, Hoot Owl, Brett's, and the 1776 Inn

"Here is a piece of history that has gone astray due to changing times, the loss of 1940 –1960 tourism, and the dying off of the old timers. Dwaarkill New York"

"Dwaarkill, New York today is a skeleton of its former self. The Hoot Owl, General Store, and 1776 Inn still exist, but nowhere near as each did in the 1940-1960 period. The General store was owned by the Brett family and it included a vehicle repair shop, USPS post office, gasoline station, meat market, and more.

Today it is still a general store, but without the repair shop, post office, and the benefits of penny candy for the local kids."

"The Hoot Owl, a bar and restaurant still exist, but not like it did in the 1940 -1950 period when Herb

owned it, and it had sawdust covered barroom floors with brass spittoons on each end of the bar, a separate dining area that doubled as a movie theatre playing Disney movies and WWII war info via Movietone News. Each fall the community would hold a festive outing on the hillside next to the building."

The 1776 Inn in the 1940-1950 periods had a 4-lane bowling alley with humans (myself for one) pinsetters; an outdoor swimming pool with high dive (where many of us learned to swim), and a multi-room motel, as well as a restaurant. The Bar area was decorated with the stuffed heads of the local animals, i.e. deer, and such. Today the

pool is gone, the bowling alley is gone, and the motel is gone. Much of the original 1776 building has been torn down and rebuilt to today's codes.

Plan on 30-minutes if just looking and a few hours if having a beer or a good meal.

Delaware and Hudson (D&H) Canal

Gravity Railroads

This canal was used for bringing coal from the mountains of Pennsylvania to the Hudson River and to New York City. The system contained *'Gravity Railroads'* from the mining area to the 108-mile long canal and its 108 locks as it dropped hundreds of feet to near sea level. The barges held coal, lumber, and concrete, each used to develop New York City and the surrounding areas.

D&H Canal,

66-80 Sullivan Street,
Wurtsboro, NY 12790
GPS 41.574256, -74.480994

D&H Canal Museum

A visit to the museum will allow you to see a mockup of the locks; a walk to and along the shore of some of the remaining locks, and the history of the how, what, when, and why the canal came into existence and why it became obsolete. There is a model of the

Gravity Railroad system, and a life-sized mockup of a canal boat cabin. Plan on two to three hours.

Delaware and Hudson Canal Museum,
23 Mohonk Road,
High Falls, NY 12440
GPS 41.825692, -74.126419

D & H Canal Park

D & H Canal Park,
58 Hoag Road,
Cuddebackville, NY 12729
GPS 41.460090, -74.601551

Depuy Canal House

Depuy Canal House permanently closed as of August 2018

Deyo Hall

This is part of the *Historic Huguenot Street District* is in New Paltz and is being used as a rental for various activities.

Deyo Hall,
6 Broadhead Ave,
New Paltz, NY 12561
GPS 41.752173, -74.086508

Dia:Beacon

Housed in a 300,000-square-foot historic Nabisco box-printing factory this art gallery features the works of artist from the 1960s period onward. Plan on two hours.

Dia:Beacon,
3 Beekman Street,
Beacon, NY 12508
GPS 41.500116, -73.982565

Discovery of Cement Marker

Brooklyn Bridge and the Statue of Liberty

While digging the D&H Canal the workers discovered special hydraulic cement that could be commercially mined and sold. The canal barges then came in handy as the means of transporting the cement to NYC where it was used to build the *Brooklyn Bridge* and the *Statue of Liberty*. Plan on 10-minutes.

Discovery of Cement marker
1300 NY-213, High Falls, NY 12440
41.827036, -74.126395

Eleanor Roosevelt Center-Val-Kill

President Franklin D. Roosevelt's wife Eleanor lived in this secluded

house. Plan on one to two hours.

Eleanor Roosevelt Center-Val-Kill, 106 Valkill Park Road, Hyde Park, NY 12538
GPS 1.763154, -73.899095

Ever Rest

Newington Cropsey Foundation

This 1830's home that was sold in 1886 to *Jasper F. Cropsey* who used it as his home and artist studio. He named it *Ever Rest* for the peacefulness that it provided him. The home is now a museum with limited entry {see the newingtoncropsey.com website}.

Newington Cropsey Foundation
49 Washington Ave,
Hastings-On-Hudson, NY 10706
40.993106, -73.881748

Furgary Fishing Village

Shacks', the 'Shantytown', 'North Dock Tin Boat Association'

This group of buildings along the Hudson River dates back to the 1800s and is also known as the *'Shacks'*, the *'Shantytown'*, and the *'North Dock Tin Boat Association'*. It was scheduled for demolition and thus, this piece of history would have been lost. The buildings are, were, used by hunters and fishermen in the past when sturgeon and shad were abundant in the Hudson River.

Lawsuits over the decades by the *'Furgarians'* resulted in the city of Hudson having jurisdiction over the properties, until Linda Mackey and Daria Merwin of the State Historic Preservation board managed to have the property designated as a National Historic District on the National Register of Historic Places.

In October of 2017 the matter has still not been settled to everyone's satisfaction, and site may still not be fully open to the public.

Furgary Fishing Village,
8 Dock Street,
Hudson, NY 12534
GPS 42.259530, -73.793647

Glynwood (Org) Farm

This is a farm that is open to those that want to learn about growing food, canning food, preserving food, and eating food. They have training programs to help people start their farms; and community events that help people understand each other and the agriculture communities and their needs.

From Official Website

> *"Glynwood is a non-profit organization serving food and farming professionals across New York's Hudson Valley. We advance regenerative agriculture in service of our natural environment, local economies and human health.*
>
> *Guided by the highest standards of ecosystem, soil, animal and community well being, Glynwood serves as a teaching venue for aspiring farmers and a test bed for regenerative farming practices. With considerations to realistic economic viability, we are training the next generation of agricultural entrepreneurs."*

Regenerative Agriculture

This is a system of different means to grow food without chemicals, and is also geared to generate CO_2 from the atmosphere and store it in the soil where it is beneficial to plant life. There is much advancement in the field and new studies are going on daily. Plan on three to four hours.

Turnoff is at….
707-577 Cold Spring-Carmel Road (NY-301)
Cold Spring, NY 10516
41.440639, -73.891392

Farm is at….
362 Glynnwood Road
Cold Spring, NY 10516
41.453709, -73.867831

Detailed instructions are on their website.

Gomez Mill House

This 1714 era house and mill is located off of US-9W in Marlboro New York.

There are tours of the house and of the *Dard Hunter Mill* (Shown). The small stream and dam provided the water for the waterwheel and for the processing of the paper being made at this location.

The house was built by *Luis Moses Gomez* an American Jewish leader and is influenced by *Dard Hunter, Martha Gruening, William Henry Armstrong, and Wolfert Ecker.* It is listed on the *National Register of Historic Places,* and is a 501(c) exempt property and is deemed to be the oldest standing Jewish dwelling in North America.

The mill demonstrations show how sheets of paper were hand-made in the using pulp and water on screening.

Plan on spending two to three hours at this attraction.

Note, in *2018* there are major repairs going on to the property, consult their website *gomez.org* for details and parking instructions. Also check for *Free Museum Entry* days on their website.

Gomez Mill House,
11 Mill House Road,
Marlboro, NY 12542
GPS 41.586572, -73.981682

Harden House

Union Free School District of Tarrytown

Old Croton Aqueduct Trail

You may not find the name *'Harden House'* on a map as the 1909 building is now the administration building for the *Union Free School District of Tarrytown*. Mr. Edward W. Harden built the Georgian brick mansion when he was a war correspondent for the New York Times. He believed in the *Maria Montessori* system of education and allowed sections of the building to be used for a kindergarten. The *Old Croton Aqueduct Trail* runs behind the building. Plan on 15-minutes for looking at the architecture.

210 Broadway
Sleepy Hollow, NY 10591
41.082865, -73.857448

Hudson River Sloop Clearwater

Great Hudson River Revival

Clearwater Festival

Closed on Saturday and Sunday this 106-foot wooden sailing vessel is being used as an environmental 'school' for those that want to learn about the Hudson River and its bounties. The organization has a website that gives recommendations on the fish and crabs of the Hudson and which can be consumed. I grew up in the area and went fishing and crabbing with my father every weekend during the summer and fall for years; the Catfish, Eels, and Crabs were plentiful and delicious. Today, due to companies polluting the land and the waterways of New York, there is a 'Do NOT EAT!' warning for the Catfish, Eels, and Crabs of the Hudson River Valley due to Mercury contamination. The Clearwater is designed after 18th and 19th century Dutch sailing sloops.

Ask about the *Great Hudson River Revival* or the *Clearwater Festival*. Plan on 30 minutes to several hours.

Hudson River Sloop Clearwater, Inc.
724 Wolcott Ave,
Beacon, NY 12508
41.489703, -73.964770

Hudson Valley Center for Contemporary Art

Hudson Valley MOCA

This is a local artist location from showing off their talent. Plan on one or more hours.

Hudson Valley Center for Contemporary Art,
1701 E Main Street,
Peekskill, NY 10566
GPS 41.293327, -73.906760

Hudson Valley MOCA
1701 Main Street,
Peekskill, NY 10566
41.293261, -73.906864

Hudson Valley Old Time Power

If you like antique equipment, auctions, tractor pulls, and lots of good old fashion fun, then perhaps this is for you. Plan on two to four hours.

Hudson Valley Old Time Power,
390 Fingar Road,
Hudson, NY 12534
GPS 42.208131, -73.780019

Indian Point Energy Center

This is the home of the first U.S. Nuclear Power Plant and it was built in the 1950s. The fact that we did not know much about earthquake

faults at the time did not come into consideration when they built the plant on the junction of two faults. Indian Point sits just one mile south of the *Stamford-Peekskill line*, part of the

Ramapo Fault Zone

(Photo from Rt 9W by Daniel Case, Wikipedia website GNU Free Documentation License)

Indian Point 1 built in 1954 has been shut down, Indian Point 2 (1974) and 3 (1976) are scheduled to shut down in 2021. The controversy is that the state depends on about 10% or more of its power from this plant and there currently seems to be no scheduled replacement. There is also concern for the Hudson River due to the heating of the water used to cool the reactors being returned to the river.

Note that boating is restricted in the area near the power plant due to national security considerations.

It does not appear that they still give tours that are open to the public as they did in the past and when first opened.

Indian Point Energy Center,
Broadway,
Buchanan, NY 10511
GPS 41.268014, -73.951399

Jacob T Walden House (Old Hearthstone)
'Kidd Town'

Walden House. Built early 1700's on 1000 acre Gatehouse Patent Purchased 1813 by Jacob T. Walden   The Wallkill (River) Powered His Textile Mills.

This house was built of cut stone and has walls that are 2-foot in thickness. The architecture is Hudson Valley Dutch Colonial, and it was built on Gatehouse Patent Land around 1768 under the land grant.

Jacob Treadwell Walden purchased the building from the Samuel

Erwin family heirs in 1813; the village at that time was named *'Kidd Town'* and it needed some industry. Walden built textile mills along the Wallkill River and used the waterfalls for generating the necessary power.

{*Photo from the thewaldenhouse.org website*}

The old powerhouse sits at the base of the *High Falls*. Eventually, the textile industry moved to other lands, and the house became a listing on the New York State and National Register of Historic Places; it is today used for Historical Society of Walden and Wallkill Valley.

The town's name was changed to Walden to honor Mr. Walden and his contribution to its growth. Plan on 10-minutes at this location.

Jacob T Walden House,
34 N Montgomery Street,
Walden, NY 12586
GPS 41.565171, -74.194834

Jay Heritage Center

1838 Peter Augustus Jay Mansion

1907 Van Norden Carriage House

Closed on Saturday, Monday, and Tuesday this center offers tours to the 1838 Peter Augustus Jay Mansion and the 1907 Van Norden Carriage House. Plan on three or more hours to do the tours.

Jay Heritage Center

210 Boston Post Road,
Rye, NY 10580
40.957321, -73.706083

Karpeles Manuscript Library

This is one of many Karpeles libraries and it is displaying portraits of famous Americans like the Indian Heroes, Pioneer, and Founding Fathers. Plan on one to two hours.

Karpeles Manuscript Library,
94 Broadway,
Newburgh, NY 12550
GPS 41.500330, -74.010529

King Mansion

Tarrytown House Estate

This 1840s mansion was named after railroad magnate Thomas King. It is one of the oldest buildings in the *Tarrytown House Estate* area. Each of the ten rooms you may visit has custom furniture and artwork for the period. The Tarrytown House Estate is a Hudson Valley Landmark and has since the 1800s been home to wealthy railroad and tobacco families.

49 E Sunnyside Lane,
Tarrytown, NY 10591
GPS 41.050992, -73.857928

Kykuit, the Rockefeller Estate

'High Point' is the English name for the Dutch name *'Kykuit'*, and this estate certainly lives up to the name as it overlooks the Hudson River.

The estate has furniture, paintings, and sculptures as well as beautiful gardens, fountains, and terraces. The Kykuit estate was built in 1902 by John Davison Rockefeller Sr. (July 8, 1839 – May 23, 1937) and was passed down to John D. Rockefeller Jr. and then to Nelson Aldrich Rockefeller (July 8, 1908 – January 26, 1979), four-time governor of New York and vice president under Gerald Ford.

John Davison Rockefeller Sr. was the creator of Standard Oil Company.

Kykuit, the Rockefeller Estate,
381 N Broadway,
Sleepy Hollow, NY 10591
GPS 41.087950, -73.862682

Lasdon Park, Arboretum & Veterans Memorial

Westchester County Park that has several different themes including a *dinosaur walkway* where you travel back 366 million years or so and duck the various dinosaurs that greet you from the bushes. You can also walk to the fountains, the military tanks, and the statues of those in battle. There are lots of water, flowers, and other items to entertain, as well as special events throughout the year. Plan on two to four hours.

2610 NY-35,
Katonah, NY 10536
41.276447, -73.737724

Locust Grove Estate

Samuel Morse who died in 1872 owned this 1852 Tuscan-style villa. The house then was rented to *William and Martha Young* who furnished it and later purchased it. Today it has miles of hiking trails, excellent views of the Hudson River, and is open as a museum that shows off the elegance of the era.

The complex has a gift shop, and an area for weddings and other events. The estate now features the Young family's painting, decorative arts, and furniture that number some 15,000. Plan on one hour.

Locust Grove Estate
2683 South Road
Poughkeepsie, NY 12601
41.672364, -73.929996

Locust Lawn Estate

Colonel Josiah Hasbrouck Estate

Evert Terwilliger House

This home below New Paltz, New York was also part of the Young family's estate properties and Annette Young moved the contents to the Locust Grove Estate. The Hasbrouck estate was part of the Terwilliger farm until purchase by Mr. Hasbrouck who built the new Federal style mansion in 1814. Plan on two hours.

Locust Lawn Estate,
436 State Route 32 South,
Wallkill, NY 12589
 GPS 41.697841, -74.101765

Lyndhurst Mansion

{Photo from Wikipedia is Public Domain}

This building of Gothic Architecture styling was the home of *Jay Gould* the railroad magnate. Two other families also lived there and the current furnishings are from the three family estates. Plan on one to two hours.

Lyndhurst Mansion,
635 S Broadway,
Tarrytown, NY 10591
GPS 41.053974, -73.867345

Manitoga / The Russel Wright Design Center

Place of Great Spirit

The Industrial designer *Mr. Russel Wright* (1904-1976) lived in this Bear Mountain area home that is listed on the National Register of Historic Places and is open to the public. Plan on one hour.

584 Route 9D

Garrison, New York 10524

Turn at:
16-22 Old Manitou Road
Garrison, NY 10524
41.349196, -73.953606

Motorcyclepedia Museum

If you remember the *'Indian'* brand of motorcycles then you will
enjoy your visit to this museum. It contains every model 'Indian'
from 1901 to 1953, as well as hundreds of other cycle brands and
models. It also has items like the 1897 De Dion-Bouton trike, and the
1901 Thomas.

(Picture from the I love New York website)

This is a 85,000-square foot
facility on two floor, so plan
on one to four hours to see it
all.

Motorcyclepedia Museum
250 Lake Street,
Newburgh, NY 12550
41.493903, -74.032624

Newburgh Brewing Company

This is housed in an old brick warehouse and brews several flavors
of beer. The place is an experience as it is rustic, entertaining, and if
you like beer, well... Plan on one or more hours.

Newburgh Brewing Company,
88 Colden Street,
Newburgh, NY 12550
GPS 41.497329, -74.007971

Newburgh Pier

Newburgh, New York is on the Hudson River and the pier area has
been used for local entertainment and festivities.

City of Newburgh Waterfront Trail
1 Washington Street
Newburgh, NY 12550
41.497859, -74.005404

Northgate, Cornish Estate

Per the Hudson Valley State Park.

> *Hudson Highlands State Park, Northgate. Popularly known as the*
> *'Cornish Estate' the ruins seen here were built by NYC Diamond*
> *Merchant Sigmund Stern in the early 1910's. The building and*
> *surrounding 650 acres were inhabited by Edward and Selina Cornish from*
> *1916 to 1938, when both dies within two weeks of each other. A fire in*
> *1958 destroyed most of the mansion. The property became part of the*
> *Hudson Highlands State Park in the late 1960's after a failed attempt by*
> *Central Hudson Gas and Electric to turn the property into a power plant.*
> *For further information please visit www.hudsonvalleyruins.org*

You have to hike in to see the ruins; the hike is mild and though a
wooded area where you will see streams and waterfalls, wildlife, and
several of the remains of the mansion. Plan on two or more hours.

Cold Spring, NY 10516
41.437856, -73.970332

Cornish Estate Trail Head

3206 Bear Mountain-Beacon Hwy
Cold Spring, NY 10516
41.426827, -73.965684

There is another building ruin along the Notch Trail that is deeper
into the woods.

Cornish Estate ruins

Cold Spring, NY 10516
41.448477, -73.963083

Old Rhinebeck Aerodrome

If you enjoy the barnstorming of the 1920s then you will enjoy the air
shows and the bi-planes that are at this facility. Plan on two or more
hours.

Old Rhinebeck Aerodrome,
9 Norton Road,
Red Hook, NY 12571
GPS 41.969371, -73.863910

Onderdonck Tallman Budke House

Jersey Dutch Stone House

This 1696 house is an example of Dutch Architecture of the era. It is considered to be a *'Jersey Dutch Stone House'*, but over the decades it was modified and currently it is being restored to the changes made by the Budke family in or around 1875. Plan on one hour.

Onderdonck Tallman Budke House,
98-130 Germonds Road,
West Nyack, NY 10994
GPS 41.117134, -73.987268

Philipsburg Manor

Closed on Monday and Tuesday this 1750 complex that supported a thriving milling and trading complex. The complex has a dam on the Pocantico River, a waterwheel driven mill, and other building used for storage and sales. The workers were mainly African Slaves, some 23 lived and worked here.

Philipsburg Manor
381 N Broadway,
Sleepy Hollow, NY 10591
41.087989, -73.862633

Philipse Manor Hall State Historic Site

Closed on Sunday and Monday this 1682 Georgian style estate features a 1750's Papier Mache Rococo Ceiling. The estate has a history in that it belonged to Frederick Philipse III who was loyal to the King of England and against the newly forming government of the United States. The property was thus confiscated and became the first Yonkers Village Hall in 1868 and then the in 1872, the first City Hall.

Today the property includes portraits of six New York State Presidents and local exhibits. Plan on one hour.

Philipse Manor Hall State
29 Warburton Ave,
Yonkers, NY 10701
40.935685, -73.899472

Rosen House

This estate house provides tours, music entertainment, a bed that once belonged to *Pope Urban VIII*, doors designed by *Giovanni Battista Tiepolo* (1695-1770), Asian and Renaissance art, items from private villas and chateaux in Italy, France, and England, and Spanish Ceilings. It is a Mediterranean-style House built in the 1929 to 1939 period of the Great Depression by German born *Walter Rosen* an International Banker that specialized in railroads. Plan on two or more hours.

Rosen House,
3815, 149 Girdle Ridge Road,
Katonah, NY 10536
GPS 41.238900, -73.647077

Scenic Hudson RiverWalk Park at Tarrytown

This is a riverfront park where you can see both the Tappan Zee Bridge and Manhattan.

Scenic Hudson RiverWalk Park at Tarrytown,
250 W Main Street,
Tarrytown, NY 10591
GPS 41.077420, -73.869229

Sculpture of Headless Horseman

Legend of Sleepy Hollow

Ichabod Crane (1820) was a character in *Washington Irving's* short story of the '*Legend of Sleepy Hollow*' and this metal statue represents Crane being chased through the woods by the *Headless Horseman*.

Sculpture of Headless Horseman,
362 Broadway,
Sleepy Hollow, NY 10591
GPS 41.088873, -73.861550

Seven Lakes Drive

This is a scenic highway that goes from the New York Route NY-17 at Sloatsburg through the Harriman State Park to the Bear Mountain Bridge. Plan on one to three hours to enjoy the drive and the mountain scenery.

Harriman State Park,
Southfields, NY 10975
41.298400, -74.049115

Shawangunk Ridge National Scenic Byway

Start at Bullville (NY-17K) and head to Pine Bush on NY-302. At Pine Bush you can go north or south, preferred is to go south on NY-52 to Walden where you turn onto Route NY-208 (Ulster Avenue) north to Wallkill and past Ireland Corners to New Paltz where you catch US-299 west. This will become US-44/US-54 just before the absolute great view of the mountains and *Gertie's Nose* ahead of you.

Going up and over the mountains you will come to NY-209 where you can turn left toward Ellenville or right toward Rosendale. The route toward Rosedale has many historic and other sites to visit, but is not as scenic as the route to Ellenville where you again join with NY-52 and travel over the mountain to Pine Bush as you pass Sams Point.

From US-209 at Stone Ridge turn east on NY-213 toward Rosendale; in Rosendale you will turn south on Keaton Avenue, which will become James and then Sand Hill Road. Take Sand Hill Road south past St. Peters Cemetery to Elting Road that will become Springtown Road south.

At Rosendale you will be on US-213, and then go south on Springtown Road (County #7) to New Paltz where you can get on the New York Thruway or go onto NY-299 west to US-44/US-55 and the mountains.

25

The entire trip is about 88 to 95 miles and without stops will take about 2 to 2.5 hours, with stops, figure one or more days as there are dozens of places to visit and turn offs with views of the mountains.

Springwood

President Roosevelt's Childhood Home

President Roosevelt's Burial Place

Not many people get to be born and then buried in the same family estate, but president Franklin D. Roosevelt did, and is at this Hudson River estate. The NPS runs the estate these days as well as the Presidential Library and Museum on the property.

The grounds that overlook the Hudson River have FDR's grave site, garden, and horse stables. Next door is the Henry A. Wallace Visitor and Education Center and the Roosevelt and Vanderbilt National Historic Site. Plan on spending most of the day at this location.

Springwood
4097 Albany Post Road,
Hyde Park, NY 12538
41.767215, -73.935566

Staatsburgh

Tales of the Titanic

Closed on Monday, Tuesday, and Wednesday this Beaux-Arts mansion of has 65 rooms and 14 bathrooms, and one would hope plenty of maids. The estate was the home of *Ruth Livingston Mills* (1855-1920) and her husband *Ogden Mills* (1856-1929).

Many of the elegant rooms were copied and duplicated on the Titanic and the Mills were claimed to have been booked on the second voyage of the ship, lucky them.

Today the mansion is open to the public, and if you ever wanted to see what the staterooms of the Titanic looked like, then here is your chance.

Staatsburgh State Historic Site

75 Mills Mansion Drive, 1 Road,
Staatsburg, NY 12580
41.856654, -73.929919

Stone Barns Center for Food and Agriculture

Once living on a farm the author is not excited by seeing some farm animals and paying to learn about some of the sustainable agriculture methods being used. But, for a *'City Folk'* type, this is an ideal way to spend a day in the country enjoying the air and the newly acquired knowledge of from where food comes. There is a small kitchen where you can get some food while there, and there are lectures on farming and things for the young folk to do that may keep them interested. Plan on two to four hours.

Stone Barns Center for Food & Agriculture
630 Bedford Road,
Tarrytown, NY 10591
41.103267, -73.824538

Stonecrop Gardens

This botanical garden has mixed reviews, some really like it, other visitors not so much.

From the Official Website

> *"At its windswept elevation of 1,100 feet in the Hudson Highlands Stonecrop enjoys a Zone 6a climate. The gardens cover an area of approximately 15 acres and comprise a diverse collection of gardens and plants including woodland and water gardens, a grass garden, raised alpine stone beds, cliff rock gardens, and an enclosed English-style flower garden. Additional features include a Conservatory, display Alpine House, Pit House with an extensive collection of choice dwarf bulbs, and systematic order beds representing over 50 plant families."*

Plan on two hours.

81 Stonecrop Lane
Cold Spring, NY 10516
41.441348, -73.869182

Storm King Art Center

To many a sculpture is a depiction of a person or animal constructed from cement, marble, steel, copper, or other material. The sculptures in this park like setting are not what one would normally expect, but more toward the geometric and distortedly flowing. PS. Look but do not touch as they are monitoring your presence and will *'Caution'* you over the loudspeakers if you do. {First hand experience}.

Plan on an hour.

Storm King Art Center,
1 Museum Road,
New Windsor, NY 12553
GPS 41.425110, -74.059384

Sunnyside

See *Washington Irving's home*

Taconic Outdoor Education Center

This is a New York State Government enterprise that has tons of activities for young adults during all seasons. Plan on several hours.

75 Mountain Laurel Lane
Cold Spring, NY 10516
41.422802, -73.879036

Tarrytown Music Hall

This 1885 Queen Anne style theater was built by the chocolate candy manufacturer *Mr. William Wallace*, and is still in operation.

The design is Art Deco and the acoustics are said to be absolutely excellent, and enough so that people like Bruce Springsteen, Dizzy Gillespie, Joan Baez, Tony Bennett, and others have entertained there. Presidents Taft, Wilson, and Roosevelt have made appearances there and since 1980 over 50 recordings have been created at the facility.

Plan on 30-minutes to view, a few hours to see a show.

13 Main Street
Tarrytown, NY 10591
41.076500, -73.858826

The Palisades Parkway Visitor Center and Bookstore

This is a rest stop about two miles south of the Bear Mountain
Bridge.

Palisades Interstate Pkwy,
Tomkins Cove, NY 10986
41.288810, -74.025593

The Temple of Virtue

New Windsor Cantonment

This 1782 building was constructed with a vaulted ceiling and large
glazed windows and was used for military functions, musical
performances, and church services. It is next to the New Windsor
Cantonment historic site where *General George Washington* stayed at
the end of the Revolutionary War. Plan on one hour.

The Temple of Virtue,
370 Temple Hill Road,
New Windsor, NY 12553
GPS 41.472896, -74.059352

Tillson Lake

Palmaghatt Kill

The *Palmaghatt Kill* feeds the lake; the dam is on the east side. The
Kill starts in the high mountains at or around *Lake Minnewaska* and
flows to the lake, and then exits the lake to flow to the *Wallkill River*
and eventually to the *Hudson River*.

Tillson Lake today is somewhat smaller than it once was, and is used
for fishing, kayaking, and canoeing.

The history of the lake dates back to the 1930's and beyond when it
was a top tourist spot at the foot of the *Shawangunk Mountains*. Back
then there was a beach, dozens of covered and uncovered tables and
seating areas, a raft off the beach by about 50 feet or more, several

dozen summer cottages, a 9-hole golf course, and a skating rink pavilion with snack bar.

Story # 1... The north side of the lake was vacant until some developer started to build and someone complained about the noise and tourist on the south side.

Lawsuits resulted and the lake's owner put a stop to it by blowing up the dam and draining the lake. It became a giant swamp for several years until the new dam was constructed.

Story # 2 See the New York Times article *'Owner pulls the plug on Ulster County Lake,* in the July of 1983

Which is the correct story? Probably both, but whichever is true, the lake never returned to its great fun and glorious days.

Top Cottage (FDR's Retreat)

Churchill and Franklin D. Roosevelt spent a peaceful evening here as they conversed about *'Heavy Water'* the item of interest at the time. Roosevelt used the stone faced building as a retreat, and had planned on retiring into it, but his being elected to a third term and dying in office ended that dream. The facility is closed in the winters, but open in the spring; it is run by the National Park Service (NPS). Plan on one hour.

Top Cottage
98 Valkill Drive,
Poughkeepsie, NY 12601
41.765089, -73.888787

Tuthilltown Grist Mill

Like many of the buildings from the 1780's period of development this too has been converted for something other than residential use. It is a restaurant that serves fine food and drink.

> *"1788 Tuthilltown Grist Mill. This continuously operated water-powered flourmill is recognized as a national historic site possessing exceptional value in commemoration and illustration the history of our nation. Registered in 1982 by the U.S. Department of the Interior"*

Around 1982 the mill started producing *Kosher Flour* used for baking Matzo. In 2007 the mill was converted into a restaurant and it opened in 2010. Plan on one hour.

1788 Tuthill House at the Mill,
20 Grist Mill Lane,
Gardiner, NY 12525
GPS 41.686929, -74.174925

Union Church of Pocantico Hills

If you enjoy the workmanship of excellent rockwork, tremendous stained glass, and ringing bells then this church may be what you seek, it has it all. Closed on Tuesdays the church will astound you with its charm and beauty. Plan on 15 minutes.

Union Church of Pocantico Hills
555 Bedford Road,
Tarrytown, NY 10591
41.095645, -73.832356

Van Cortlandt Manor

The Manor of Cortlandt

Open Friday, Saturday, and Sunday this estate dates back to when in 1697 by King William III granted 86,000-acres to *Stephanus Van Cortlandt*. The building was built around 1732, but not moved into by Mr. Cortlandt until 1749. The estate has a history during and after the Revolutionary War and remained in the family until purchased by Otis Taylor, in 1945. Plan on one hour.

Van Cortlandt Manor
525 S Riverside Ave,
Croton-On-Hudson, NY 10520
41.191656, -73.876505

Vanderbilt Mansion

This is one of *Frederick W. Vanderbilt's* homes; it is a 54-room mansion in Hyde Park, New York. Frederick William Vanderbilt (February 2, 1856 – June 29, 1938) loved making money in the railroad business and was the director of the Pittsburgh and Lake Erie Railroad, the Chicago and North Western Railroad, and the New York Central Railroad.

The National Park Service owns and runs this estate and provides tours of the rooms and the furnishings of it.

Plan on two or more hours.

Vanderbilt Mansion National Historic Site,
119 Vanderbilt Park Road,
Hyde Park, NY 12538
GPS 41.796359, -73.942385

Villa Lewaro

Madam C. J. Walker

> *"In Honor of Madam C. J. Walker 1867 - 1919 the first African American Millionairess and a great philanthropist. In 1917 she made Villa Lewaro her home.. George E. Pataki, Governor."*

This villa reminds one of Hurst Castle in that much of the architecture is similar. Plan on one hour.

Villa Lewaro,
67 N Broadway,
Irvington, NY 10533
GPS 41.043178, -73.863989

Washington Irving's Sunnyside

When you arrive at Sunnyside you will enter a ticket office / gift shop on the top of the hill overlooking the Hudson River.

We got there behind a group of others that wanted to take the tour, and we had a choice of guides from which to select. The group chose the young well dressed guides, we the older gentleman that was dressed in very out of date black clothing, with cane, and top hat *(Shown)*.

The other tour left first and was done in about 20 minutes. Our tour that consisted of four plus the guide took over an hour. Why, well our guide was the 'reincarnation' of Washington Irving, or so it seemed. He acted the part, lived the period, and kept us entertained and educated about the Irving home and its past occupant, which made it a very enjoyable and informative visit.

Mr. Irving wrote the *'Legend of Sleepy Hollow'*, *'Rip Van Winkle'* and many other books and magazines. He was the first America recognized for his authorship works by the British and European communities.

Plan on one to two hours with wait time and browsing the gift store.

Washington Irving's Sunnyside,
3 W Sunnyside Lane,
Irvington, NY 10533
GPS 41.047803, -73.868541

Widow Jane Mine

Snyder Estate, Century House Historical Society

Snyder Estate Natural Cement Historic District

Rosendale Cement was mined here and you can visit the small museum where you may learn about the mine, see some of the mining equipment, and then take the short walk to the mine. Note that during certain times of the year the mine is pretty wet, and to some it becomes a subterranean lake. You may require a good flashlight and some walking shoes that are suitable for mud and water.

Look for the Snyder Estate, Century House Historical Society sign for entry. Plan on two hours or more.

Widow Jane Mine,

668 NY-213,
Rosendale, NY 12472
GPS 41.842322, -74.098652

Wilderstein

Wild Man's Stone

Closed Monday, Tuesday, and Wednesday this Victorian estate was
the home of FDR's distant cousin *Margaret (Daisy) Suckley* who lived
to be 100. Ms. Suckley was the person that gave FDR his dog Fala.

John Warren Ritch designed this Italianate country home in 1852; and
the interior was partly done by *Joseph Burr Tiffany* of New York.

The name *"Wilderstein"* translates to *"Wild Man's Stone"* and referred
to a Petroglyph found on a stone on the property.

Wilderstein Historic Site
330 Morton Road,
Rhinebeck, NY 12572
41.894046, -73.942136

Woodstock Farm Sanctuary

Open only on Saturday and Sunday.
From the official website.

> *"Woodstock Farm Sanctuary envisions a peaceful world rooted in respect
> and justice for all living beings."*

> *"We rescue farmed animals and give them care and sanctuary, connect
> animals with people to advance veganism, and advocate for animal rights
> in alliance with other social justice movements."*

> *"We welcome visitors to come and meet animals who are most commonly
> exploited, abused, and killed in animal agriculture. Our animal residents
> are given lifelong sanctuary and are treated with respect as individuals."*

Plan on one hour or more.

Woodstock Farm Sanctuary
2 Rescue Road,
High Falls, NY 12440

Chapter # 02 ... Beaches

The Hudson Valley and the surrounding mountains provide many rivers and lakes that can be used for boating, floating, fishing, and swimming. The following is a listing of some of the beaches where one can escape from the heat of the city, and enjoy a day surrounded by nature. Note that the 'Locals', especially along the Wallkill River, have many 'unmarked' swimming areas. Just ask, and you shall find quiet and out of the way spots.

Bar Beach

Fishing, swimming & sports facilities

Bar Beach
Port Washington, NY 11050
40.829344, -73.655328

Bear Mountain Park & Beach

Bear Mountain Park is known for the *Bear Mountain Inn* and the *Bear Mountain Bridge*. The small lake near the inn is a popular spot for beating the New York summer's heat. {Shown}

From the New York State Parks Website {parks.ny.gov}:

> *Bear Mountain State Park is situated in rugged mountains rising from the west bank of the Hudson River. The park features a large play field, shaded picnic groves, lake and river fishing access, a swimming pool, Trailside Museums and Zoo, hiking, biking and cross-country ski trails. An outdoor rink is open to ice skaters from late October through mid-March. The Perkins Memorial Tower atop Bear Mountain affords spectacular views of the park, the Hudson Highlands and Harriman State Park. Perkins Memorial Drive and Tower are open from April through late November, weather permitting.*

There is also a merry-go-round with hand painted and carved animals. Dogs are permitted in the park, but must be on a 6 foot or less leash and are restricted to locations, see the parks website for more info.

Bear Mountain Park & Beach
55 Hessian Drive,
Bear Mountain, NY 10911
GPS 41.320355, -73.996702

Kingston Point Beach

Kingston Point Beach
102-144 Delaware Ave,
Kingston, NY 12401
41.930123, -73.964760

Lake MacGregor Beach

238 Beach Drive
New York 10541
41.379717, -73.770409

Lake Tiorati Beach

2350 New York State Reference Rte 987E,
Southfields, NY 10975
41.275155, -74.087693

Lake Welch Beach

Sandy beach on a man-made swimming lake

Lake Welch Beach
800 Kanawauke Road,
Stony Point, NY 10980
41.234970, -74.073008

Minnewaska Lake Beach

Scuba Diving lessons have been provided in this lake over the years. There are several lakes in the Shawangunk Mountain chain, but this is the only one with a beach area and parking. While there, spend

the day and take the walk around the lake; on the far end you will
have excellent views of the Hudson Valley far below.

Minnewaska Lake Beach
Gardiner, NY 12525
41.727463, -74.237824

Nyack Beach State Park

River park with trails & boat launches

Nyack Beach State Park
698 N Broadway,
Nyack, NY 10960
41.120789, -73.911327

Saugerties Village Beach

Saugerties Village Beach
47 S Partition Street,
Saugerties, NY 12477
42.071131, -73.951268

Sylvan Lake Beach Park Inc

Sylvan Lake Beach Park Inc
18 McDonnell's Lane,
Hopewell Junction, NY 12533
41.604514, -73.745404

Chapter # 03 ... Bridges

The Hudson River is only one of the main rivers in the Hudson
Valley; there are several including the Wallkill and other creeks and
streams. The following is a listing of bridges that cross the Hudson
River, and includes a covered bridge that crosses the Wallkill River.

Bear Mountain – Purple Heart Bridge

The *Bear Mountain Bridge* is one of the few in this area that crosses the
Hudson River. It is a toll bridge and for decades collected a fee for
those crossing it, until it became too unsafe for vehicle traffic due to
having nearly none of the collected fees used for maintenance,
especially paint that should have protected the steel. The bridge was

closed for a few years as they replaced rusted out portions and then painted it. Those needing to cross the Hudson therefore had nearly a 50-mile 'detour' during this period. Hopefully, the authorities learned their lesson and the bridge will remain safe for decades into the future.

Bear Mountain,
55 Hessian Drive,
Bear Mountain, NY 10911
GPS 41.320355, -73.996702

Castleton-on-Hudson Bridge

NY-912M
Schodack Landing, NY 12156
42.508753, -73.771333

Congress Street Bridge

Watervliet, NY 12189
42.729201, -73.698459

Kingston-Rhinecliff Bridge

NY-199
Kingston, NY 12401
41.980866, -73.955970

Newburgh-Beacon Bridge

NY-52/I-84
Newburgh, NY 12550
41.521061, -74.007667

Perrine's Covered Wallkill River Bridge

Perrine's Covered Bridge - Wallkill River
New Paltz, NY 12561
41.817501, -74.055443

Poughkeepsie Bridge

This was a railroad bridge that crossed the Hudson River. It was abandoned by the railroads and became in disrepair over the years until the townships decided to make it a tourist attraction. You can walk the bridge from Lloyd to Poughkeepsie and thus, get magnificent views of the Hudson, the New York Central tracks, and the towns.

Poughkeepsie Bridge,
Walkway Over the Hudson,
Poughkeepsie, NY 12601
GPS 41.710623, -73.945840

Purple Heart Memorial Bridge

See *Bear Mountain Bridge*

Rip Van Winkle Bridge

99 NY-23,
Catskill, NY 12414
42.224612, -73.855507

Tappan Zee Bridge

Governor Malcolm Wilson Tappan Zee Bridge

Governor Mario Cuomo Tappan Zee Bridge

This 4.5 mile long toll bridge has recently been built, the original was too small for the traffic volume and falling apart due to its age. {~ 64 years as it was competed in 1955}

I-287
Tarrytown, NY 10591
41.065289, -73.865154

Chapter # 04 ... Campgrounds

Although not far from New York City and other major urban areas, the Hudson Valley for decades was mostly farmland. It was dotted with apple orchards, dairy farms, and truck farms {Potatoes, and other vegetables}. It also was abundant in fruit and nut trees, and berries of many kinds that could be picked as one walked the rural roads. Over the years the local highway departments killed off the berries, the apple orchards grew unproductive, the dairy farms were replaced by dairy giants elsewhere, and the truck farms replaced by housing developments.

Today it is a changed area and thus much of the valley has been converted to State and Local Parks, vineyards, and campgrounds. Here are some of the more popular tenting campgrounds, see elsewhere in this manual for RV camps. NOTE: Check carefully as some of these camps are 'Children's' camps, and not for adults.

Agatha A. Durland Scout Reservation

Agatha A. Durland Scout Reservation
1 Clear Lake Road,
Putnam Valley, NY 10579
41.410752, -73.837195

Beaver Pond Campground

Beaver Pond Campground
700 Kanawauke Road,
Stony Point, NY 10980
41.232376, -74.067289

California Hill State Forest

Rugged forest for hunters & explorers

California Hill Road
Carmel Hamlet, NY 10512
41.438609, -73.777081

Camp Bullowa

15 Franck Road
Stony Point, NY 10980
41.245127, -74.002699

Camp Combe YMCA

Nonprofit center for classes & services, with a Zip Line.

Camp Combe YMCA
684 Peekskill Hollow Road,
Putnam Valley, NY 10579
41.395790, -73.804525

Camp Floradan

Camp Floradan
40 Floradan Road,
Putnam Valley, NY 10579
41.349409, -73.869118

Camp Hillcroft

1562 State Rte 55
Lagrangeville, NY 12540
41.668237, -73.758844

Camp Lakota Sleepaway & Summer Camp Upstate NY

Camp Lakota Sleepaway & Summer Camp Upstate NY
56 Park Road,
Wurtsboro, NY 12790
41.609083, -74.536530

Camp Nabby

Camp Nabby
1 Nabby Hill,
Mohegan Lake, NY 10547
41.311720, -73.844572

Camp Olmsted

Religious Retreat center

106-128 NY-218
Cornwall-On-Hudson, NY 12520
41.440601, -74.002425

Camp Redwood

Camp Redwood
576 Rock Cut Road,
Walden, NY 12586
41.571889, -74.115325

Camp Yachad

Camp Yachad
8 Bedford Court,
Spring Valley, NY 10977
41.131723, -74.055467

Canopus Beach Complex

Sandy beach, campsites, hiking & more

Canopus Beach Complex
1498 NY-301,
Carmel Hamlet, NY 10512
41.471351, -73.823560

Challenge Camp

555 W Hartsdale Ave
Hartsdale, NY 10530
41.032656, -73.808139

Clarence Fahnestock State Park

Vast area with trails, a beach & more
Check to see if open, it was closed for maintenance

Clarence Fahnestock State Park
1498 NY-301,
Carmel Hamlet, NY 10512
41.465690, -73.836367

Durland Scout Reservation

Turnoff to the camp by the lake that is about a mile up the road.
1 Clear Lake Road
Putnam Valley, NY 10579
41.408668, -73.836549

Eden Village Camp

Eden Village Camp
392 Dennytown Road,
Putnam Valley, NY 10579
41.413096, -73.865079

Fahnestock State Park Campground

Fahnestock State Park Campground
Clarence Fahnestock State Park,
Putnam Valley, NY 10579
41.465988, -73.824136

Green Chimneys Summer Camp - Hillside

Green Chimneys Summer Camp - Hillside
400 Doansburg Road,
Brewster, NY 10509
41.454767, -73.552438

Group Sites 1 & 2

Group Sites 1 & 2
Dennytown Road,
Putnam Valley, NY 10579
41.421149, -73.868958

Henry Kaufman Camp

Sunrise Day Camp-Pearl River
44 Henry Kaufmann Road,
Orangeburg, NY 10962
41.063900, -73.990818

John V Mara Valley Camp

John V Mara Valley Camp
197 Peekskill Hollow Road,
Putnam Valley, NY 10579
41.342060, -73.852663

Kiwi Country Day Camp

Kiwi Country Day Camp
825 Union Valley Road,
Carmel Hamlet, NY 10512
41.360738, -73.687650

Malouf's Mountain Campground

Malouf's Mountain Campground

Beacon, NY 12508
41.507608, -73.921859

Marist Brothers Center at Esopus

Marist Brothers Center at Esopus
1455 Broadway,
Esopus, NY 12429
41.814736, -73.959771

Putnam Valley Parks and Recreation

Putnam Valley Parks & Recreation
Oscawana Lake Road,
Putnam Valley, NY 10579
41.367979, -73.866139

Rock Hill Camp

Rock Hill Camp
300 Wixon Pond Road,
Mahopac, NY 10541
41.407742, -73.731295

Rosmarin Day Camp

Rosmarin Day Camp
11 School Road
Monroe, NY 10950
41.299450, -74.220333

Sam Pryor Shawangunk Gateway Campground

953 NY-299,
Gardiner, NY 12525
41.731970, -74.185603

Surprise Lake Camp

382 Lake Surprise Road
Cold Spring, NY 10516
41.455631, -73.955683

Sylvan Lake Beach Park Inc

Sylvan Lake Beach Park Inc
18 McDonnell's Lane,
Hopewell Junction, NY 12533
41.604511, -73.745413

Wayfinder Experience Inc.

Wayfinder Experience Inc
61 Oneil Street
Kingston, NY 12401
41.931773, -74.004090

Wild Earth

Wild Earth
2307 Lucas Turnpike,
High Falls, NY 12440
41.828692, -74.135120

YMCA Camp Wiltmeet

YMCA Camp Wiltmeet
Lenape Elementary School,
1 Eugene L Brown Drive,
New Paltz, NY 12561
41.709942, -74.093515

Chapter # 05 ... Climbing Areas

There are a few commercially built indoor climbing areas; the
following are outdoor natural climbing areas that will challenge the
beginner as well as the seasoned professional.

Bonticou Crag

Bonticou Crag
This is a mountain outcropping of rock that is almost directly north
of New Paltz. The mountain area has several hiking trails and places
for rock and mountain climbing, and is popular with climbers.

New Paltz, NY 12561

41.788081, -74.118840

Gunks at the Mohonk Preserve

Folks from New York City and the suburbs can fly to Yosemite to do some rock climbing, or they can drive an hour or so to the *'Gunks'* a rock climber's heaven less than a hundred miles from the city.

The *Mohonk Preserve* has this spectacular outcropping of rock that attracts some 50,000 climbers per year, which makes it the greatest concentration of quality beginner and intermediate climbs to be found anywhere in the world.

Good quality rock, lots of handholds, challenging roofs, and access from the nearby Route 44/55 and the local trails adds to the attraction.

The Trapps and the Lost City

> *"The Trapps and Near Trapps crags are the most popular, with about two miles of white cliffs up to 250 feet high. The cliffs of "Lost City" are in the backcountry."*

Peter's Kill Area

> *"At the Peter's Kill Area, the Minnewaska State Park Preserve offers the only technical rock climbing of any of the state parks in New York, with access for 65 climbers at a time"*

NOTE: See the gunksclimbers.org website before setting out to climb, they monitor the bird nesting in the area, and due to the birds many areas may be 'off-limits' for climbing.

Ramapo Powerlinez

Ramapo Powerlinez
250 Torne Valley Road
Hillburn, NY 10931
41.143808, -74.160464

Trapps Cliffs

The Trapps, Gardiner, NY 12525
GPS 41.736927, -74.191929

Wallkill Valley Overlook - Gertrude's Nose

Gertie's Nose

Hannah McElroy coined the phrase back in 1944 as she looked out of her 1880's farmhouse window while talking to her girlfriend *Gertie Kellner*. The rock formation that was miles distant almost exactly resembled Gertie's facial profile, and thus the name was penned and has persisted for decades.

Wallkill Valley Overlook,
Main Street,
Gardiner, NY 12525
41.735856, -74.192417

Chapter # 06 … Graves & Burial Plots

Andrew Carnegie Grave

Mr. Carnegie shown here was born in 1835 in Fife, Scotland. He died 11 Aug 1919 (aged 83) and is buried in the Sleepy Hollow Cemetery.

{1913 Picture is Public Domain from Theodore C. Marceau - Library of Congress}

Mr. Carnegie is best known as the founder of the *United States Steel Corporation* (known today as the USX Corporation).

Toward the end of his life he became a philanthropist and donated millions to the education of those that wanted to attend his namesake colleges. In 1960 he was awarded the *Carnegie Endowment for International Peace* award for founding the Carnegie endowment.

He was on the 4-cent stamp and has a stain glass window at the National Cathedral in Washington, D.C. and has the following named for him due to his generous contributions.

>Carnegie Vanguard High School
>Carnegie Library at Syracuse University
>Carnegie Library, Macomb, Illinois
>Carnegie Library, Hornell, NY
>Carnegie Hall, New York City.
>Carnegie Mellon University
>1906 Yorkville Library, Ontario.

Andrew Carnegie Grave,
Sleepy Hollow, NY 10591
GPS 41.096418, -73.860045

Samuel Gompers Grave

American Federation of Labor

Cigar-Makers Union

This cigar-maker founded the *American Federation of Labor* in 1886, and he was the president of the *Cigar-Makers Union*.

Samuel Gompers Grave,
Sleepy Hollow, NY 10591
GPS 41.096566, -73.860736

Washington Irving Grave

He who wrote about Sleepy Hollow in 1820 is resting forever in the soil of the town of Sleepy Hollow.

Washington Irving Grave,
Sleepy Hollow, NY 10591
GPS 41.091791, -73.861466

William Rockefeller Mausoleum

From Wikipedia

William Avery Rockefeller, Jr. (May 31, 1841 – June 24, 1922) was an American businessman and financier. He was a co-founder of Standard Oil along with his older brother John Davison Rockefeller (1839–1937).

William Rockefeller Mausoleum,
Sleepy Hollow, NY 10591
GPS 41.097638, -73.859751

Chapter # 07 ... Hiking Trails

See Chapter on *Railroads & Rail Trails* for some that use old torn out railroad beds for hiking. The Hudson Valley is somewhat hilly, mountainous, and very much covered with a variety of trees and flora, thus making it ideal for hiking in the warmth of the summer and fall. Winters and springtime present a challenge, but many will use the hiking trails for 'snowmobiling' or cross-country skiing. In the spring the land can be wet, flooded, and somewhat dangerous at times, so beware.

Also be aware that both rattlesnakes and copperheads are plentiful in the area, thus take proper precautions while hiking, camping, etc.

Note that many trails do NOT begin at roadside parking lots, thus you will need to generate maps using the GPS provided with the names.

1777 Trail

Tomkins Cove, NY 10986
41.276241, -73.992761

Anthony Wayne Loop Trailhead

Tomkins Cove, NY 10986
41.298354, -74.027777

Anthony's Nose Trail Head

171-143 Bear Mountain-Beacon Hwy,
Garrison, NY 10524
41.322593, -73.975946

Appalachian Trail

Seven Lakes Drive,
Tomkins Cove, NY 10986
41.304061, -74.013291

Appalachian Trail Genesis

Appalachian Trail,
Tomkins Cove, NY 10986
41.311032, -74.006706

Appalachian Trail NJ-NY Border

Appalachian Trail, Hewitt, NJ 07421
41.192467, -74.342923

Appalachian Trail Parking/ Tiorati Circle

Arden Valley Road,
Southfields, NY 10975
41.275265, -74.088900

Cat Rocks

Appalachian Trail, Warwick, NY 10990
41.263599, -74.270120

Fingerboard Shelter

Appalachian Trail,
Southfields, NY 10975
41.263309, -74.104045

Fitzgerald Falls

Appalachian Trail,
Southfields, NY 10975
41.271073, -74.251185

Wildcat Shelter

Appalachian Trail,
Warwick, NY 10990
41.268654, -74.268241

Anthony Wayne Loop Trailhead

Tomkins Cove, NY 10986
41.298377, -74.027774

Arden Surebridge Trail (red markers)

Southfields, NY 10975
41.256991, -74.147712

Bear Mountain–Harriman State Park

Bear Mountain Doodletown Circuit

Bear Mountain Hike Trail

Tomkins Cove, NY 10986
41.313297, -73.988647

Blue Mountain Reservation Loop

Blue Mountain Reservation,
Cortlandt, NY 10567
41.272011, -73.924123

Blue Mountain Trail

Blue Mountain Reservation
Peekskill, NY 10566
41.272441, -73.924133

Blue Trail – New Paltz

New Paltz, NY 12561
41.837557, -73.994142

Boston Mine Trail

Southfields, NY 10975
41.246346, -74.146114

Boundary Trail

Blue Mountain Reservation
Cortlandt, NY 10567
41.272228, -73.922991

Breakneck Ridge Bypass Trail

Cold Spring, NY 10516
41.453909, -73.966185

Breakneck Ridge Trail

Cold Spring, NY 10516
41.443273, -73.977726

Brook Trail

Cold Spring, NY 10516
41.438223, -73.972474

Castle Point Trail

Unnamed Road
Gardiner, NY 12525
41.725390, -74.237675

Colden Trail

Rock Tavern, NY 12575
41.515124, -74.165181

Constitution Marsh Trail

Warren Landing Road
Garrison, NY 10524
41.401395, -73.938027

Cornell Mine Trail Head

Stony Point
New York 10986
41.300438, -73.985977

Cornish Trail

Cold Spring, NY 10516
41.427292, -73.965632

Coxing Trail

Gardiner, NY 12525
41.720327, -74.219779

Croton Reservoir Walking Trail

595 Saw Mill River Road,
Yorktown Heights, NY 10598

41.231688, -73.779818

Dawn Trail

Montgomery, NY 12549
41.515276, -74.165135

Doodletown Trail Head

Stony Point
New York 10986
41.300803, -73.985916

DP(R) Trail Access

West Kill, NY 12492
42.159624, -74.203345

Escarpment Trail

Rock Tavern, NY 12575
41.506416, -74.183262

Fanny Reese State Park Trails

Highland, NY 12528
41.703348, -73.951741

Gertrude's Nose / Minnewaska Trail

5281 Route 44-55, Kerhonkson, NY 12446
41.730422, -74.234406

Goethals Trail – West Point

West Point, NY 10996
41.384341, -73.992128

Green Trail – Ulster Park

Ulster Park, NY 12487
41.841354, -73.997358

Hamilton Point Trail

Gardiner, NY 12525
41.727491, -74.238245

Hickory Hollow Road/Trail

Tuxedo Park, NY 10987
41.243822, -74.204327

High Point Carriageway

Ellenville, NY 12428
41.719603, -74.338411

Horse Trail Yellow

Rock Tavern, NY 12575
41.506688, -74.174849

Howell Trail

Cornwall-On-Hudson, NY 12520
41.432700, -73.992626

Hunter Brook/Ox Hollow Trail

Unnamed Road
West Kill, NY 12492
42.187892, -74.269834

Indian Head Mountain Loop

Devil's Path
Elka Park, NY 12427
42.116237, -74.114575

Japan Trailhead

1184-1340 Kanawauke Road,
Southfields, NY 10975
41.229063, -74.143442

Jeep Trail

Kerhonkson, NY 12446
41.720799, -74.325974

Kingston Point Rotary Park Trails

Unnamed Road
Kingston, NY 12401

41.928427, -73.967441

Ladentown Mountain Trail

Pomona, NY 10970
41.201713, -74.088987

Long Path (aqua markers)

Southfields, NY 10975
41.267054, -74.117062

Lower Awosting Carriageway Parking Lot

Old Minnewaska Trail,
Kerhonkson, NY 12446
41.734635, -74.244269

Major Welch Trail Head

Major Welch Trail,
Tomkins Cove, NY 10986
41.318331, -73.994218

Millbrook Mountain Path

Gardiner, NY 12525
41.716544, -74.230296

Millbrook Mountain Trail

Gardiner, NY 12525
41.708395, -74.225997

Minnewaska Lake Trail Head

Gardiner, NY 12525
41.729460, -74.235179

Minnewaska State Park Preserve

This is an extremely popular park with a lower and an upper level section for campers, hikers, swimmers, scuba divers, and nature lovers. The park entry road is winding and twisting as it takes you to the top of the mountain, but is well maintained. The lake has a hiking path the surrounds it, and there are several places to sit if you get too exhausted. Bring sunscreen, camera, water, food, and watch out for snakes.

The trails are labeled and color-coded; but getting on the wrong trail can take you all the way to *Mud Pond*, which is a decent hike of many miles; thus remember which trail you are on and keep to it.

Minnewaska State Park Preserve
5281 Route 44-55,
Kerhonkson, NY 12446
41.730073, -74.235299

Mohonk Hiking Parking Lot

High Falls, NY 12440
41.779241, -74.136236

Mohonk Preserve Spring Farm Trailhead Parking

4147 N 39th Street,
High Falls, NY 12440
41.795490, -74.127499

Mohonk Preserve West Trapps Trailhead Parking Area

3142 US-44, Gardiner, NY 12525
41.736086, -74.200341

Moneyhole Mt. Trail

774-700 Indian Brook Road,
Garrison, NY 10524
41.418520, -73.898526

Mossy Brook Trail

Mohonk Road
High Falls, NY 12440

Muskrat Trail

Rock Tavern, NY 12575
41.506963, -74.172354

N County Trailway

Yorktown Heights, NY 10598
41.234225, -73.782680

North County Trail Park

284 Saw Mill River Road #254,
Yorktown Heights, NY 10598
41.231002, -73.778898

N Lookout Trail

High Falls, NY 12440
41.782212, -74.135380

Notch Trail

Cold Spring, NY 10516
41.455626, -73.962863

Nurian Trail (White N markers)

Southfields, NY 10975
41.235763, -74.143666

O&W Trail Parking

O&W Rail Trail, Cottekill, NY 12419
41.855090, -74.107502

Old Croton Aqueduct Trail

Tarrytown, NY 10591
41.081584, -73.856758

Old Ski Trail

Tomkins Cove, NY 10986
41.291851, -73.997223

Orange Trail – New Paltz

New Paltz, NY 12561
41.836284, -73.999209

Panther Mt. Trail

Oliverea Road,
Big Indian, NY 12410
42.026665, -74.403720

Peekamoose-Table Trail Head

Peekamoose Road
Grahamsville, NY 12740
41.915119, -74.428828

Pine Meadow Road/Trail

Pine Meadow Road
Pomona, NY 10970
41.197248, -74.105422

Pine Root Trail

Rock Tavern, NY 12575
41.506857, -74.172660

Pipeline Trail

West Point, NY 10996
41.393413, -73.987270

Plum Point Park Trails

Unnamed Road
New Windsor, NY 12553
41.462584, -74.012581

Rainbow Falls Trail - Wallkill

Wallkill, NY 12589
41.712739, -74.273341

Rainbow Falls Trail - Kerhonkson

Jenny Lane,
Kerhonkson, NY 12446
41.742600, -74.254391

RD Trail

Tuxedo
New York 10975
41.230936, -74.140255

Red Trail – New Paltz

New Paltz, NY 12561
41.837626, -73.994177

Red Trail - Highland

Highland, NY 12528
41.716448, -73.981553

Roosevelt Farm Lane Trail

4088 Albany Post Road,
Hyde Park, NY 12538
41.771391, -73.928980

Sams Point Fat/Foot, Road/Trail

Ellenville, NY 12428
41.670582, -74.360771

Sawmill Trails

Mohonk Road
High Falls, NY 12440
41.782146, -74.135177

Scofield Lane Trail Orange

Rock Tavern, NY 12575
41.489055, -74.164729

Shaupeneak Ridge Lower Parking Lot/White Trail

Ulster Park, NY 12487
41.827166, -73.970237

Slide Fall

Napanoch, NY 12458
41.722712, -74.362108

Slide Mountain Loop

Slide Mountain Trailhead Parking Lot
2099 Oliverea Road,
Big Indian, NY 12410
42.008040, -74.428290

Smiley Carriageway

Kerhonkson, NY 12446
41.711044, -74.293980

Spring Farm Trailhead parking

Marbletown, NY 12440
41.795514, -74.127507

Sterling Lake Loop

Sterling Lake Corp,
Tuxedo Park, NY 10987
41.198905, -74.256842

Sterling Ridge Trailhead

797 Minturn Bridge Road
Monroe, NY 10950
41.230418, -74.260785

Stony Kill Carriageway (Abandoned)

Kerhonkson, NY 12446
41.714490, -74.320106

Suffern - Bear Mountain Trail

Tomkins Cove, NY 10986
41.305861, -73.999904

Tanbark Trail, Phoenicia, NY

6 St Ursula Place,
Phoenicia, NY 12464
42.085087, -74.311923

Timp Torne Trailhead

Ramapo-Dunderberg Timp Torne Trail,
Tomkins Cove, NY 10986
41.281053, -73.962900

Trapps Trail - Undercliff Road

Undercliff Road
Gardiner, NY 12525
41.737069, -74.194923

Undercliff Trail -Gardner

Undercliff Road
Gardiner, NY 12525
41.736834, -74.193907

Undercliff Trail –Cold Spring

Cold Spring, NY 10516
41.445972, -73.971567

Upper Awosting Carriageway - Wallkill

Wallkill, NY 12589
41.712676, -74.273346

Upper Awosting Carriageway - Gardiner

Hamilton Point Trail
Gardiner, NY 12525
41.727495, -74.238316

Verkeerderkill Falls Trail

Cragsmoor, NY 12420
41.674184, -74.350533

Wallkill Valley Rail Trail

River Road Extended
New Paltz, NY 12561
41.820046, -74.085224

Washburn Trail

7357 Louisiana 57,
Cold Spring, NY 10516
41.427020, -73.966006

Wawarsing Turnpike Trail

Kerhonkson, NY 12446
41.740821, -74.251601

White Bar trailhead

Southfields, NY 10975
41.235067, -74.149151

White Trail – New Paltz

New Paltz, NY 12561
41.841076, -73.985421

White Trail - Highland

Highland, NY 12528
41.726834, -73.985532

Yellow Trail – New Paltz

New Paltz, NY 12561
41.837557, -73.994142

Yellow Trail - Highland

Highland, NY 12528
41.726766, -73.985550

Chapter # 08 … Historic Buildings/ Sites & Markers

The state of New York, especially the Hudson Valley area is one of the first places settled by the British; that is after the decades of Native Americans and folks from other lands. The Dutch also settled there and they too claimed the land and built homes and mansions from the native rock and lumber. Thus, today you will find buildings dating back into the 1600's and beyond that qualify a 'National Historic Sites'. These sites are now considered tourist attractions and although many are NOT open to the public, many are and have been converted into museums, restaurants, education centers, and art centers.

Abigail Kirsch at Tappan Hill Mansion

Hillcrest

Tappan Hill Mansion

This 1882 building is known as *Hillcrest* and dates back to the days of George Washington; it has a much history.

The estate was purchased by *Mark Twain* in 1902 and sold it in 1904 to Charles Gardner who sold it to Jacques Halle in 1915. It is known locally as the *Tappan Hill Mansion* and it overlooks the Hudson River.

In season it has beautiful gardens and is a favorite location for weddings and other ceremonies in the lower Hudson Valley.

{Picture is a snippet from the abigailkirsch.com website}

Abigail Kirsch currently owns the property and she is the caterer for many of the weddings at this location. The property became an events location in 1990 when she took it over.

The history is that the village assessed the estate, a mansion with horse stables, too high and Mr. Twain therefore protested, and then sold. The attorney, Gardner purchased it and sold it to Halle a member of the New York Stock Exchange. Halle demolished the mansion and built a bigger mansion and named it Halleston. Halle's wife lived in the mansion until a developer by the name of David Swope purchased it and named it Tappan Hill. Ms. Kirsch then obtained it and turned it into the restaurant it is today.

Abigail Kirsch at Tappan Hill Mansion, 81 Highland Ave, Tarrytown, NY 10591 - GPS 41.071942, -73.853661

Clermont State Historic Site

From the ILoveNY website.

> *"Ancestral home and estate of Robert R. Livingston, who drafted the Declaration of Independence, negotiated the Louisiana Purchase and teamed up with Robert Fulton to develop the first steamboat the North River Steamboat later, know as "the Clermont"."*

The building dates back to the 1740/1750 period when America was being created, and seven (7) generations of the Livingston family lived here. Today it is managed by the State of New York and provides tours during certain times of the year. The grounds overlook the Hudson River and are a favorite place for those just wanting a 'claiming' day's rest.

Plan on two or more hours.

Clermont Manor
Clermont State Park,
Germantown, NY 12526
42.085960, -73.919158

Huguenot Street National Historic Landmark

THE OLD DU BOIS HOUSE OR FORT IN THIS VILLAGE

Historic Huguenot Street This town on the Wallkill River was purchased (Negotiated) from the *Esopus Indians* and then built of native stone and lumber. It is located in New Paltz, New York about 90 miles north of New York City, and short distance from the New York State Thruway. This is now a 10-acre Historical District and it contains seven houses and several other buildings.
{Picture is Public Domain}

64

Plan on a full day in New Paltz to see this street and all the houses, as well as the other attractions of the area.

The following identifications come from the official website, please consult it for more details, dates each building can be seen, and for any tours they offer.

1799 House

"1799 House... Built by Ezekiel Elting as a home and store, original Gambrel Roof destroyed in 1888 blizzard. 1968 purchased by Le Fevre family assoc. Maintained by HHS and Le Fevre Family."

Bevier-Elting House (1698)

Bevier-Elting House (1698) in the Huguenot Street National Historic Landmark District, one of 56 listings on the National Register. "Bevier House built by Louis Bevier. The Patentee, in 1698. Elting Homestead from 1740. This house has an interesting sub-cellar."

Burying Ground

"Burying Ground. Crispell Memorial French Church"

Deyo House

"Deyo House... built by Pierre Deyo, one of the Twelve Original Patentees of New Paltz in 1692"

Die Pfalz

Die Pfalz.. A French Huguenot village governed by "The Dusine". A body of 12 men chosen annually. For 100 years the only form of government"

Die Pfalz was an area in Germany where these people escaped from religious persecution before moving to *New Netherland* {America}

Dubois House

"Dubois House... The fort built in 1705 by Daniel Dubois. Site first redoubt. There are Port Holes in the East end. "

Freer House

{Not open to the public}

French Church 1717

"French Church 1717. Rebuild 1972 in memory of Antoine Crispell Patentee by his descendants."

Hasbrouck House

"Built in 1712. By Abraham, the Patentee, once soldier in English Arm. Friend of Gov. Andros. Kitchen scene of Cock Fights"

Jean Hasbrouck House

"Jean Hasbrouck house built in 1712, by Patentee; Now home of the Huguenot Patriotic Historical and Monumental Society, since 1899"

New Paltz

"New Paltz. Founded in 1678. Six houses built before 1720 are on Huguenot Street on the Wallkill River. Homes of Refugees from France"

Stone Church 1773

"Stone Church - 1773... First Stone Church, 1717. Services in French to 1753, Dutch Language to 1800. Church Corner Stone seen at south wall of Portico."

Walloon Church

"Sit of the Walloon Church built of Logs, First church-school, 1682. First church of Stone 1717. Called "Our French Church" precursor reformed church"

Historic Huguenot Street

81 Huguenot Street,
New Paltz, NY 12561
GPS 41.751656, -74.088394

John Jay Homestead Historic Site

Bedford House

This 1801 house was the home of *Mr. John Jay*. For those not familiar with Mr. Jay, he was the first Chief Justice of the United States.

Mr. Jay (1745-1829) co-authored the *Treaty of Paris*, the *Federalist Papers*, and was one of the Founding Fathers of our nation.

(Picture is Public Domain)

66

Mr. Jay was president of the *Continental Congress*, and was the second governor of New York State.

Your visit to the estate may include an 1820;s schoolhouse, and an 1830's barn as well as the several farm buildings, the main house, and the formal gardens and paths. Plan on two to three hours.

John Jay Homestead,
400 Jay Street,
Katonah, NY 10536
GPS 41.251813, -73.660253

Martin Van Buren National Historic Site

Lindenwald

This mansion was the home of *President Martin Van Buren*, the eighth President of the United States.

{Photo from National Park Service, NPS - Public Domain}

Martin Van Buren was a one-term president and is credited as being the founder of the Democrat Party. He purchased the estate in 1839 while serving as President, and it become his retirement home after his presidency in 1841. Plan on two hours.

Martin Van Buren National Historic Site,
1013 Old Post Road,
Kinderhook, NY 12106
GPS 42.369815, -73.704191

Montgomery Place Historic Estate

Bard College - Montgomery Place Historic Estate

See the write-up on the Clermont State Historic Site and the Livingston family. This estate belonged to members of the family from 1802 to 1986. Today it is part of the Bard College campus, and is open to the public. Plan on one or more hours.

Bard College

Campus Road, PO Box 5000
Annandale-on-Hudson
New York 12504-5000

Montgomery Place Historic Estate
26 Gardener Way
Red Hook, NY 12571
42.014580, -73.918965

Mount Gulian Historic Site

Mount Gulian, after the fire.

{Photo after the 1931 arson fire, from the mountgulian.org website}

This site dates back to the 1680's. During the Revolutionary War the building served as the headquarters of Major General Friedrich Wilhelm von Steuben.

The Society of the Cincinnati was founded here. The building is thought to have been modified, expanded, in the 1730/1740 periods and again in the 1767 period. In 1931 it was burnt by an arsonist and remained a ruin for several decades until rebuild in 1975. Today it is open for tours. Plan on one to two hours.

Mount Gulian Historic Site,
145 Sterling Street,
Beacon, NY 12508
GPS 41.523604, -73.980015

Nevele Old Hotel Historical Landmark

The Nevele is a decades old resort just west of Ellenville, New York. It was in the 1940-1950s the 'resort' for the elite from New York City that came to the Catskills for relaxation.

State Route 52 brought people from the city to the *'Borscht Belt'* where comedians and entertainers flourished. The advent of jet

68

passenger aircraft in the late 1950s and the new Route 17 highway took much of the business from the area, and it almost died over the next few decades.

("Borscht Belt, or Jewish Alps, is a nickname for the (now mostly defunct) summer resorts of the Catskill Mountains in parts of Sullivan, Orange, and Ulster counties in New York", Wikipedia)

Nevele Old Hotel Historical Landmark,
Ellenville, NY 12428
 GPS 41.698004, -74.402051

Olana State Historic Site

Open Friday, Saturday, and Sunday only, this home of artist *Frederic Edwin Church* (1826-1900). The 1870's estate sits high on a hill overlooking the Hudson River at Catskill. Plan on one hour or more.

Olana State Historic Site,
5720 NY-9G,
Hudson, NY 12534
GPS 42.217270, -73.829298

Perkins Memorial Tower

This tower is off the Appalachian Trail near Bear Mountain and provides great views of the Hudson River, the bridge, and on a clear day the NYC skyline. Note that you can enter and climb the stairs to the observation area at the top, but beware that it is glassed in and taking pictures may result in getting pictures of your reflection and not the scenery.

Per Wikipedia
> *"The road and tower were built by the Civilian Conservation Corps between 1932 and 1934. It is named after George Wallbridge Perkins, the first president of the Palisades Interstate Park Commission"*

Plan on 30-minutes to an hour. Note that you can hike or drive to the tower.

Perkins Memorial Tower,
Perkins Memorial Drive,
Stony Point, NY 10980

GPS 41.311524, -74.006913

Staatsburgh State Historic Site

Closed Monday, Tuesday, and Wednesday this American
Renaissance, the Gilded Age (1876-1917) era Beaux-Arts mansion
belonged to *Ogden Mills* (1856-1929) and his wife *Ruth* (1855-1920) of
the Livingston family.

Per the NYS Parks Commission Website

> *"In the 1890s Mr. & Mrs. Mills commissioned the prestigious New York
> City architectural firm of McKim, Mead and White to remodel and enlarge
> their home. Work began in 1895 and when completed in 1896, the house
> had been transformed from a 25-room Greek Revival style home into a
> Beaux-Arts mansion of 65 rooms and 14 bathrooms. Although the interior
> was lavishly decorated, mostly in the styles of 17th and 18th-century
> France, many architectural features of the earlier Livingston home such as
> the all the trims, moldings and many of the fireplaces had been preserved."*

Plan on two or more hours.

Staatsburgh State Historic Site
75 Mills Mansion 1 Road,
Staatsburg, NY 12580
GPS 41.856659, -73.929925

Thomas Cole National Historic Site

Open on Saturday and Sunday only this
Mr. Thomas Cole was an artist that produced excellent landscape
artworks and this was his home; there are displays of his lifestyle and
work throughout. Plan on one hour.

Thomas Cole National Historic Site,
218 Spring Street,
Catskill, NY 12414
 GPS 42.225780, -73.861501

Thomas Jansen House

*"A distinctive example of 18th century stone architecture unique to Dutch
settlers in Ulster County. Rear Wing 1727 Main House 1780"*

70

This house is on Jansen Road in Pine Bush, New York. It is one of several homes still standing and occupied from the 1700 era.

There are other homes in the area that are not stone, but lumber

instead. The lumber is all hand-cut as are the beams, and each beam is put together with pegs. No nails were used to create the frameworks. Floorboards were sawed from the local tree stock and in some homes still have flooring with the original bark.

The National Register of Historic Places buildings are not open for tours as people reside in each, but you can view the architecture from the roads, i.e., Jansen Road, Awosting Road, and Decker Road.

Torne Monument

Popolopen Torne

This is a makeshift monument to POW (Prisoners of War) and MIA (Missing in Action) service members. It is on top of a hill by Bear Mountain and is a pile of rock with remembrances sprinkled throughout.

You have to hike to the monument and it is along a fairly difficult trail over and on mostly rocks. Not recommended for the very young of old. Plan on two hours.

Highland Falls, NY 10928
41.327268, -74.010407

Popolopen Torne Parking
288 Mine Road,
Highland Falls, NY 10928
41.324225, -74.007565

Chapter # 09 ... Historical Societies

There are Historical Societies throughout the U.S., and volunteers that believe that the loss of history is harmful to our nation and the children of our future. These citizens work hard to preserve the history of buildings, places, and things and deserve our respect.

Many of the Historical Societies have preserved more than one location and many will provide tours to various historic sites, just ask. Here are a few of the Historical Societies that dot the Hudson Valley.

Century House Historical Society

Widow Jane Mine

This is the entry to the *Widow Jane Mine*.

Century House Historical Society,
668 NY-213,
Rosendale, NY 12472
GPS 41.840981, -74.097719

Friends of Historic Kingston

Open Friday and Saturday only this is a group that provides tours of the various historic places in Kingston, New York.

Friends of Historic Kingston,
63 Main Street,
Kingston, NY 12401
GPS 41.932455, -74.019602

Historical Society Newburgh

This group provides tours of the various historic places in Newburgh, New York

Historical Society Newburgh,
189 Montgomery Street,
Newburgh, NY 12550
GPS 41.508771, -74.008153

Historical Society of Rockland County

Closed Monday, Tuesday, and Saturdays this group provides tours of the various historic places in Rockland County and the Hudson Valley, New York

Historical Society of Rockland County,
20 Zukor Road,
New City, NY 10956
GPS 41.171071, -73.986713

Historical Society-Middletown

Closed on Wednesdays this group provides tours of the various historic places in and around Middletown, New York

Historical Society-Middletown,
Middletown, NY 10940
GPS 41.444390, -74.417836

Chapter # 10 ... Lighthouses

The Hudson River in the 1800's was a major waterway from NYC to

Albany and part of the *Delaware & Hudson Canal system*. Thus, it was traveled day and night, in clear weather and nasty foggy weather; lighthouses helped keep the shipping channels free of accidents and the grounding of the cargo barges.

Hudson Athens Lighthouse

{Wikipedia photo, Author Kafziel, is in Public Domain}
Congress spent $35,000 in 1872 to have this *'Middle Ground Flats'* lighthouse constructed. The lighthouse was built to warn Hudson River shipping of the low water hazards.

In 1874 the construction was completed and the U.S. Coast Guard manned the lighthouse until the 1950s when it was automated, but still under their control until 1984 when it became a leasehold to the *Hudson-Athens Lighthouse Preservation Society, Inc.*

In July of 2000 the lighthouse officially became the sole property of the *Hudson-Athens Lighthouse Preservation Society, Inc.*

Hudson Athens Lighthouse,
Hudson, NY 12534
GPS 42.251987, -73.808682

Rondout Lighthouse

This lighthouse is open for tours; a solar powered boat will take you to it.

1915 Hudson River Lighthouse
Hudson River
41.920893, -73.962523

Saugerties Lighthouse

1869 Hudson River Lighthouse

Saugerties Lighthouse,
168 Lighthouse Drive,
Saugerties, NY 12477
GPS 42.072049, -73.929693

Hudson River location
42.072006, -73.929807

Sleepy Hollow Lighthouse

1880's Sleepy Hollow Lighthouse,
Tarrytown Light-Kingsland Point Path,
Sleepy Hollow, NY 10591
GPS 41.084054, -73.874246

Stony Point Lighthouse

Closed on Saturday and Sunday.

Per the NY State Park Commission website

"Visit the site of the Battle of Stony Point, one of the last Revolutionary War battles in the northeastern colonies. This is where Brigadier General Anthony Wayne led his corps of Continental Light Infantry in a daring midnight attack on the British, seizing the site's fortifications and taking the soldiers and camp followers at the British garrison as prisoners on July 16, 1779."

"The site features a museum, which offers exhibits on the battle and the Stony Point Lighthouse, as well as interpretive programs, such as reenactments highlighting 18th century military life, cannon and musket firings, cooking demonstrations, and children's activities and blacksmith demonstrations."

1826 Stony Point Lighthouse
46 Battlefield Road,
Stony Point, NY 10980
41.241386, -73.971744

Lighthouse Park and Historical Marker

Shoreline park with access to the *Esopus Meadows Lighthouse.*

255 River Road,
Ulster Park, NY 12487
41.868433, -73.951227

Esopus Meadows Lighthouse

1871 Hudson River Lighthouse
Hudson River
41.868404, -73.941641

Chapter # 11 ... Military History Sites

Camp Shanks World War II Museum

Last Stop USA

Shanks Village

During WWII many were drafted or volunteered to serve in the military of the US, and Camp Shanks in Orangetown, New York became the camp where those going overseas were to meet and embark; thus getting the nickname the *'Last Stop USA'*.

The camp became the largest U.S. Army embarkation camp in the nation, and for some reason was named after *Major General David Carey Shanks* (1861-1940). The 2,040 acre camp held some 50,000 servicemen and women and during its days of operation processed 1,300,000 including ~ 75% of those that fought in the D-day battles.

In 1945 parts of the camp became a POW camp for German and Italian prisoners, and after the war it became a housing area for Veterans with Families that were attending the New York City universities under the GI Bill. The camp became known as *Shanks Village* at that time and was eventually closed in 1954. The current museum was opened in 1994.

The address is the Public Library building; you need to park behind the library and then go to the Quonset hut buildings to the right side of the parking lot.

20 South Greenbush Road,
Orangeburg, NY 10962
GPS 41.045209, -73.946432

Edmonston House

This 1755 house managed by the National Temple Hill Association and the town-owned *Last Encampment* is open as a museum in certain months and at select times of the week.

It is said that the home was used by *General Horatio Gates* and *Arthur Saint Clair* during the Revolutionary War, and that it many also have been used as a Continental Army medical staff headquarters. These claims have been disputed, and therefore one must consider both claims when visiting the property.

Edmonston House,
1061-1029 NY-94
New Windsor, NY 12553
41.453322, -74.061253

Fort Montgomery

This 1972 National Historic Landmark has a visitor's center, trails, and interpretive signs that guide visitors through the fort's ruins. The visitor's center is also the museum that contains a model of the fort, artifacts, and mannequins that represent the military that once served there.

The site along with *Fort Clinton* on the east bank of the Hudson was selected due to its access to the narrows of the Hudson River that could be used to prevent enemy ships from proceeding north of the location. A giant Chain was connected between the two forts and it was thought to be strong enough to stop the ships of the day long enough for the 70 cannons to open fire and sink the intruders.

The Continental Army established the fort in 1776 during the Revolutionary War. The fort was originally planned as *Fort Constitution* miles north of this spot near *Bear Mountain*, but it was found that the spot was unsuitable, and thus moved to its current location under the name of *Fort Montgomery*.

Fort Montgomery,
690 US-9W,
Fort Montgomery, NY 10922
GPS 41.323900, -73.987360

Knox Headquarters

{Photo from Wikipedia, author Daniel Case 2006-07-01, it is used under license}

This 1754 Georgian – Dutch style house was built for the Ellison family of which *John Ellison* was a prosperous merchant.

Nathanael Greene and *Horatio Gates* used the house as a headquarters toward the ending of the Revolutionary War.

It also was used as a headquarters for *General Henry Knox* in 1779 and the winters of 1780 and 1781. Plan on one hour.

Knox Headquarters,
289 Old Forge Hill Road,
New Windsor, NY 12553
GPS 41.455124, -74.049755

National Purple Heart Hall of Honor

Closed on Mondays this facility honoring our heroes is located at the *New Windsor Cantonment site*.

National Purple Heart Hall of Honor,
374 Temple Hill Road,
New Windsor, NY 12553
GPS 41.471785, -74.058662

New Windsor Cantonment State Historic Site

'George Washington Slept here' are signage that appear throughout the Hudson Valley, and this folks is one of the actual places. It was the last place General Washington lived before the end of the Revolutionary War.

Today it is a State Historic site where you can learn the history of the encampment, see people in costume, and watch people work as they did during the Revolutionary War period when some 8,000 soldiers and their families lived and worked here. Plan on two to six hours.

New Windsor Cantonment State Historic Site,
374 Temple Hill Road,
New Windsor, NY 12553
GPS 41.471476, -74.058951

Washington's Headquarters State Historic Site

Closed on Monday and Tuesdays this house served as a headquarters for General George Washington and his aids from 1782 to 1783

Washington's Headquarters State Historic Site,

84 Liberty Street,
Newburgh, NY 12550
GPS 41.497722, -74.009925

West Point Military Academy

Battle Monument

This U.S. Army military college was established along the shores of the Hudson River in 1802.

The grounds have many canon and other items that date back for decades, and there is an excellent museum where one can see the weapons and uniforms of those that served over the decades.

The complex has classroom buildings, a theater, a stadium, a hospital, a chapel, and a parade ground. Plan on seeing the Chain Battery, Thayer Hall, the parade grounds, and Statue of *General Tadeusz Kosciuszko* while touring the facility. Plan on two to four hours.

Battle Monument,
West Point, NY 10996
GPS 41.394712, -73.956837

Constitution Island

This is across the river from West Point and has a battery and the east shore chain anchoring; the chain was strung across the river to slow down enemy warships while the gun batteries on both sides of the Hudson pounded the warships into submission.

Constitution Island, United States Military Academy,
2110 New South Post Road,
West Point, NY 10996
GPS 41.402344, -73.951364

Forts of West Point

Not much remains of each of these 1778-1790 forts that dotted the land now considered part of West Point. *Picture from the dmna.ny.gov website.*

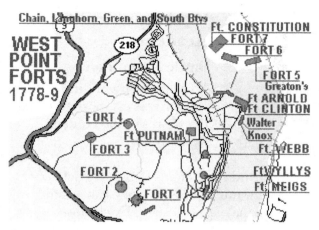

Fort Putnam

This 1778 fortress was built to support and protect Fort Clinton, both of which were at West Point years before the academy was built.

Fort Putnam, Delafield Road,
United States Military Academy,
West Point, NY 10996
41.390145, -73.963876

West Point Academy

This is the prime reason for West Point; it is the U.S. Army's college for training officers for command.

West Point Academy,
2107 New South Post Road,
Highland Falls, NY 10928
GPS 41.373093, -73.962479

West Point Foundry Preserve

Foundry Brook and waterfall was used for the manufacture of ammo for the military. There are some ruins left at the site that is just north of Constitution Island on the east side of the Hudson.

West Point Foundry Preserve,

80 Kemble Ave,
Cold Spring, NY 10516
GPS 41.415070, -73.948467

West Point Museum

This is off New South Post Road and just behind the West Point
Visitors Center where you can book tours of the complex.

West Point Museum,
2110 New South Post Road,
West Point, NY 10996
GPS 41.372661, -73.961784

South Battery - West Point

This is near the tennis courts, ball fields, etc, and is near Chain
Battery.

South Battery - West Point,
603 Cullum Road,
West Point, NY 10996
GPS 41.393382, -73.952510

Chapter # 12 … Museums

The Hudson Valley is rich in past artifacts that date back into the
1600's and many of the old mansions and farmhouses have been
converted into museums that provide education, history, and
enjoyment to millions that visit the Hudson Valley area each year.
This chapter provides the reader with suggested museums to visit
depending on the visitor's taste and curiosity, enjoy.

Brick House Historical Museum

Closed on Sunday and Monday this 1768 home was the home to
seven generations of the Hill family. Irishman *Nathaniel Hill* was
born in 1705 and helped settle the Orange County region. Mr. Hill
died in 1780 and his family lived in and maintained the home for
seven generations afterward. Some of the original furnishings,
including some Chippendale items, are in the house and on display.
The family has allowed the county to use the surrounding owned
land as a park; the *Orange County Farmers Museum* is on this park like
land. Plan on one or more hours.

Brick House Historical Museum,
Route 17 K, Montgomery, NY 12549,
Montgomery, NY 12549
GPS 41.527156, -74.177692

Bronck House Museum

Pieter Bronck House

Closed on Mondays and Tuesdays the museum caretaker is the *Green County Historical Society*. The building is said to be the oldest surviving building in Upstate New York as it dates back to 1663. The Architecture is based on Dutch and Swedish Colonial, but it has been added to more than once over the decades. Plan on one hour.

Bronck Museum
90 Co Hwy 42,
Coxsackie, NY 12051
42.345574, -73.846624

D&H Canal Museum

Open on Saturday and Sunday only this museum has the history of the D&G canal and replicas and models of the barges and canal locks. Plan on one hour.

Delaware and Hudson Canal Museum
23 Mohonk Road,
High Falls, NY 12440
GPS 41.825692, -74.126419

Edward Hopper House Museum & Study Center

Closed on Monday and Tuesdays this museum displays works of various artists. *Edward Hopper* (1882-1967) is an American Artist who lived in the house his grandfather built in 1858 until his, Edward's, death in 1910.

Edward Hopper House Museum & Study Center,
82 N Broadway,
Nyack, NY 10960
GPS 41.093287, -73.917971

Fireman's Firefighting Museum

From the Days of *Peter Stuyvesant* in 1647 and the establishment of the first volunteer firemen, to the works of *Currier and Ives* and their *'The Life of a Fireman'* the history of the fire department and fire fighters are displayed. There are depictions of the bucket brigades of the 1600's and equipment like the horse-drawn fire fighting wagons, and steam powered pumpers.

Be sure to read their **Hours and Admission page** on their website, it not only provides information on dates and time of openings, but also valuable information on bringing children and family discounts. Ask about the *Jr. Firefighter challenge* for children that meet their requirements. Note that there are also 'security' procedures that must be followed, and there is a short movie that is required to be seen, before entry.

They also have a Gift shop and Internet Sales.

117 Harry Howard Ave.
Hudson, NY 12534
GPS 42.256489, -73.779389

Foundry School Museum

Closed on Mondays and Tuesdays this museum features items about the West Point Foundry and the school used to educate the workers of the foundry in the 1830's. There are paintings by John Ferguson Weir and ironwork like the Parrott gun that was produced at the foundry. Plan on one hour.

Putnam History Museum
63 Chestnut Street
Cold Spring, NY 10516
41.416816, -73.950405

Frances Lehman Loeb Art Center Museum

This art center and museum is famous for being one of, if not the first, built as part of a university in the United States. Vassar College from 1861 to 1969 was strictly a Woman's Educational facility. Today it is coed.

The 1864 art center is used for teaching students at the college, and as a public museum that features artwork from around the world, including that of grand masters like *Albrecht Dürer* and *Rembrandt van Rijn*.

The 18,000 plus works include photographs, textiles, paintings, sculptures, glass and ceramic wares, as well as drawings, prints.

The museum's current configuration was designed by César Pelli spreads over 36,000 square feet. It is named after *Frances Lehman Loeb*, a member of the Class of 1928 who was a prime donor for its development.

Frances Lehman Loeb Art Center,
124 Raymond Ave,
Poughkeepsie, NY 12604
GPS 41.686058, -73.897469

Franklin D. Roosevelt Presidential Library and Museum

Up until President Roosevelt, the papers and other memoranda of a president went to his estate or elsewhere and thus, vaporized into the atmosphere to never be seen again.

Roosevelt in 1938 decided that his papers that dealt with his term in office should be stored for prosperity, and thus in June 30, 1941 the Presidential Library was established. What President Roosevelt failed to consider was the Second World War and his being elected to a 3rd and 4th term. The library with some 50,000,000 items proved to be too small to hold it all.

The taxpayers via the Federal Government in June 30, 2013 invested $17.5 million dollars to produce the new state-of-the-art permanent museum that is visited by thousand in Hyde Park, N.Y.

Since 1941 there have been 15 Presidential Museums built, the listing is on the National Archives Website under "Visit Presidential Libraries and Museums".

Franklin D. Roosevelt Presidential Library and Museum
4079 Albany Post Road,
Hyde Park, NY 12538
GPS 41.768706, -73.934061

Fred J. Johnston Museum

Van Leuven Mansion

Open on Friday and Saturday this 1812 Federal style house is chock full of antiques from over the lifespan of Mr. Johnson who was a professional antique dealer. The museum has eight rooms of 18th and early 19th century furnishings for your review. Plan on one hour.

AKA the Van Leuven Mansion
Friends of Historic Kingston
63 Main Street,
Kingston, NY 12401
41.932418, -74.019597

Garrison Art Center Museum

From Official Website

> *"HE RIVERSIDE GALLERIES at Garrison Art Center consists of three exhibition spaces. Each year the galleries feature a number of exhibitions that include solo shows, curated group shows, juried shows and several educational exhibitions."*

The museum features permanent exhibits along with floating exhibits and provides artwork for adults and children to enjoy.

Garrison Art Center
23 Garrisons Landing,
Garrison, NY 10524
41.382564, -73.947112

Harness Racing Museum & Hall

Goshen New York has been home to harness racing since 1838 when the *Good Time Park* track opened as the home of *Hambletonian 10*; the ancestor of all American *Standardbred horses*. The track is considered the oldest in the nation and is listed as a National Historic Landmark.

{Picture is from Wikipedia, author Kafziel, it is Public Domain}

The museum is housed in a 1913 wooden stable that has been since updated to its current status.

Per Wikipedia

> *"Exhibits include more than 1,700 paintings, lithographs and sculptures, 19,300 photographs, hundreds of drivers' uniforms, 75 sulkies, 59 sulkies and 7 carts, and a preserved stable which serves as a walk-through display case for racing equipment. The museum also maintains a research library with more than 4,000 books and videos on the sport of harness racing. The Hall of Fame is contained within the museum."*

Harness Racing Museum & Hall,
240 Main Street,
Goshen, NY 10924
GPS 41.404256, -74.319384

Haverstraw Brick Museum Inc

At one time the town of Haverstraw New York was considered the *Brick Capital of the World* and it supplied millions of bricks that were shipped down river to the new city called New York City.

{Picture is Public Domain, it shows the town buried in the 1906 landslide caused by the removal of clay from the hillsides}

The landslide destroyed homes and cost the lives of 19 residents. At the time there were some 40 brickyards dating back to the 1880's making 300,000,000 bricks per year.

September 27, 2018 the museum was closed for renovations, so consult their website for the Grand Opening, and the dates and times you can visit.

Haverstraw Brick Museum Inc.,
12 Main Street,
Haverstraw, NY 10927
GPS 41.196405, -73.963865

Hessel Museum of Art

From the I Love NY website

> *"Presenting exhibitions of contemporary art year-round on Bard's Hudson River campus. The permanent collection includes works by Janine Antoni, Sol LeWitt, Robert Mapplethorpe, Bruce Nauman, Cindy Sherman, Christopher Wool, and others. Permanent installations include works by Martin Creed, Olafur Eliasson, Robert Gober, and Lawrence Weiner."*

Hessel Museum of Art,
33 Garden Road,
Annandale-On-Hudson, NY 12504
GPS 42.020297, -73.914197

Hill-Hold Museum

Open Friday, Saturday, and Sunday this 1769 farm complex has a one-room schoolhouse, a summer kitchen, a smoke house, barn, stone farmhouse, and an herb garden for your enjoyment into an era when things were more peaceful, but hard work for those that lived the times.

Plan on two or more hours.

Hill-Hold Museum,
128 NY-416,
Campbell Hall, NY 10916
GPS 41.466509, -74.272800

Hudson Highlands Nature Museum

Consult their website for dates and times of opening; this is a child friendly area that is used to instruct about the ecology of the Hudson Valley. Plan on one or more hours at each location.

Hudson Highlands Nature Museum
120 Muser Drive,
Cornwall, NY 12518
GPS 41.422292, -74.034049

Outdoor Discovery Center

120-100 Muser Drive
Cornwall, NY 12518
41.422519, -74.034083

Wildlife Education Center

Cornwall-On-Hudson
New York 12520
41.437482, -74.016276

Hudson River Maritime Museum

This maritime museum is actually on the Rondout Creek just before it enters the Hudson River. The museum is close to the Trolley Museum, so plan on a full day of sightseeing.

The museum has many historic boat models, dioramas, history of the Hudson River and Henry Hudson, a 1898 steam engine driven tugboat, and several maps of the area used by fur traders. You also can purchase tickets to the nearby lighthouse.

Hudson River Maritime Museum
50 Rondout Landing,
Kingston, NY 12401
GPS 41.918883, -73.980935

Hudson River Museum

Glenview Historic Home Tour

Nybelwyck Hall

Closed on Mondays and Tuesdays this museum is in a castle like building that is worth visiting just for the building's architecture.

There is a planetarium and many galleries to visit, and you will be delighted by the artwork displays and other attributes. It is a family-friendly museum and there are elevators for those in wheelchairs, or otherwise handicapped.

Glenview Historic 1887 Home Tour

> *"Glenview was built by John Bond Trevor, a highly successful stockbroker, who, like many other businessmen of the late 19th century, preferred to live in comfort in the newly accessible suburbs of New York City."*

Nybelwyck Hall Doll House

> *"Nybelwyck Hall is a veritable Lilliputian house for all ages, with 24 rooms that bear colorful names like the Egyptio-Tudor Room, the Gothic Library, and the Cathedral of the Lost Souls."*

Hudson River Museum,
511 Warburton Ave,
Yonkers, NY 10701
GPS 40.954131, -73.896352

Katonah Museum of Art

Closed on Mondays, open at noon on Sundays this museum is a non-collecting institution. It relies on traveling exhibitions from artist of all cultures, disciplines, and historic periods. There is a learning center and the museum caters to young children that may someday be aspiring artist. Plan on one hour.

Katonah Museum of Art,
134 Jay Street
Katonah, NY 10536
GPS 41.262331, -73.673146

Klyne Esopus Museum

This is a small local museum housed in an old church building; it displays the history of the Esopus area and the town. Plan on 30-minutes.

764-776 Broadway
Ulster Park, NY 12487
41.853756, -73.969298

Madam Brett Homestead Museum

{Photo from Wikipedia, author Rolf Müller, used per license}

This 1709 villa is considered to be the oldest homestead in Dutchess County. Several generations of the Brett family lived here.

There are seventeen rooms to explore, each filled with paintings, books, porcelain, and furnishings of the period. Plan on one hour.

Madam Brett Homestead Museum,
50 Van Nydeck Ave,
Beacon, NY 12508

Montgomery Village Museum
Wesley Hall

This museum is across the street from the *Orange County Firefighter Museum*, it displays items of interest in the establishment of the Village of Montgomery.

{Photo from the villageofmontgomery.org website}

The museum is in *Wesley Hall*, built in 1828 as a Methodist Church. Village Historian Marion Wild procured the building in 2008 and moved the town's museum items into the building.

Plan on 45-minutes

Montgomery Village Museum,

142 Clinton Street,
Montgomery, NY 12549
GPS 41.526210, -74.235546

Museum at Bethel Woods

Closed on Mondays and Tuesdays this museum features items from the infamous Woodstock Festival days of the 1960s and 1969 festival. Plan on three hours or more.

200 Hurd Road,
Bethel, NY 12720
41.697699, -74.880777

1969 Woodstock Festival

200 Hurd Road,
Swan Lake, NY 12783
41.700973, -74.880582

Museum Village

Open Saturday and Sunday only this attraction has been around for

generations. It contains several buildings that represent the typical towns of the 1700 period of our nation.

Additionally, there is a *Gem* display under Black Light, and the Macedon building that has a *Mastodon* found in the soils of the area.

Plan on spending three to four hours or more.

Museum Village,
1010 NY-17M,
Monroe, NY 10950
GPS 41.345157, -74.199751

Napanoch Train Station Museum

Permanently Closed as of April 2019

The Neversink Valley Museum of History and Innovation

Lenape Native Americans

Open on Sunday afternoons, and by appointment on Fridays and Saturdays this museum has displays of the D&H canal, Orange County Archaeology, and the *Lenape Native Americans*. Additionally, there are history of the pre-Hollywood movie shot days when the area was used by production companies for making films. There is also a Blacksmith shop and you may learn about the art. Plan on two or more hours to see everything and walk along the canal.

The Neversink Valley Museum of History and Innovation,
26 Hoag Road,
Cuddebackville, NY 12729
GPS 41.458669, -74.603060

Orange County Farmers Museum

This museum is located behind the Brick House Museum on NY-17k and you should plan on seeing both while there. The Farmers museum is open on Saturdays and Sundays and has displays of antique farm equipment that was used by Dairy and Truck farmers of the region. Plan on two or more hours.

Orange County Farmers Museum,
167 Ward Street,
Montgomery, NY 12549
 GPS 41.526035, -74.233805

Orange County Firefighter Museum

This museum is across the street from the Montgomery Village Museum and you should plan on visiting both while there. The museum has displays of firefighting equipment and over 200 years of county firefighting is featured. Plan on one hour.

Orange County Firefighter Museum,
141 Clinton Street,
Montgomery, NY 12549
GPS 41.526000, -74.235692

Putnam History Museum

Foundry School Museum

Closed on Mondays and Tuesdays this museum is on the *West Point Foundry site* where military cannons and some locomotives were built. There website has a virtual tour that you can view to see if you want to see the exhibits in person. Plan on one hour.

Putnam History Museum,
63 Chestnut Street,
Cold Spring, NY 10516
GPS 41.416817, -73.950405

Quarryman's Museum

Opus 40

Mr. Fite worked on this acreage for nearly 40 years until his untimely death by accident. The complex is a Bluestone Quarry that he purchased, and then over the years carved and created a beautiful complex of paths and pools with fountains. The museum has tools of the trade and other items of his life.

Note: There is a discrepancy in the address, Google says 42 Fite Road, AAA and other sites say it is 50 Fite Road. The author prefers to use the Google tm, address. Plan on one hour.

42 Fite Road
Saugerties, NY 12477
42.050018, -74.032193

Samuel Dorsky Museum of Art

Closed on Mondays and Tuesdays this SUNY New Paltz museum features the artworks of local artist. Plan on one hour or more

Samuel Dorsky Museum of Art,
2447, 1 Hawk Drive,
New Paltz, NY 12561
GPS 41.740736, -74.083774

Sullivan County Museum

Closed on Mondays. If you are a historian you will absolutely enjoy this museum and the tons of eclectic items selected from the various history of the county. Items range from civilian to military, kitchens to bedrooms, and everything in-between. The visit is worth one to two hours of your time.

Sullivan County Museum,
265 Main Street,
Hurleyville, NY 12747
GPS 41.739340, -74.673051

Time and the Valleys Museum

1930s Lost Catskill Farm

Open Thursday to Sunday this museum tells the story of the farmers and country folk that lost their farms in the 1930's when the state decided to build massive water conduits for bring water to NYC from the mountains. There are several buildings on the site, including a 1870's barn, power plant, milk house, outhouse, waterwheel powered workshop, and the farmhouse. Plan on one to two hours.

Time and the Valleys Museum
332 Main Street
Grahamsville, NY 12740
41.848955, -74.549570

Van Wyck Homestead Museum

Open for tours on Saturday and Sunday this 1732 home was taken over during the Revolutionary war for Washington's supply depot in the area, and it also served as a makeshift court for a period. The home was visited by General George Washington, by the Marquis Lafayette, by Alexander Hamilton and others of fame during the period of the late 1700's. Plan on one hour.

Van Wyck Homestead Museum
504 U.S. 9,
Fishkill, NY 12524
41.523072, -73.889096

Velocipede Museum

From the motorcyclepediamuseum.org website.

> *"The Velocipede Museum, formerly Located in New Castle D.E., is a showcase of velocipedes, boneshakers, bicycles and tricycles dating from the 1860s to the 1960s. Look, learn and explore the evolution of bicycles in this latest extension of Motorcyclepedia!"*

Open on Saturdays only, plan on one hour minimum.

Velocipede Museum,
109 Liberty Street,
Newburgh, NY 12550

GPS 41.498870, -74.010860

Walter Elwood Museum

Closed on Saturdays and Sundays; taxidermy, dollhouses, weaving, and much more are on display at this small local museum. Plan on one hour or more.

Walter Elwood Museum,
100 Church Street,
Amsterdam, NY 12010
GPS 42.939594, -74.184871

Chapter # 13 ... Parks

Much of the land in the Hudson Valley is wooded, or swamp, or rocky, or otherwise not really susceptible to medium or large scale housing or industrial projects. The local town, city, county governments along with the environmentalist and State of New York have intelligently bought up these areas and converted each to parklands that can be enjoyed by all ages. There is a short-listing of some of the parks that dot the Hudson Valley area.

Minnewaska State Park

When you enter the park you drive up the hill to the very top and the parking lot. From there you have several well marked trails that circle the lake with other trails that proceed across the ridges to Sam's Point.

As you walk the trails you will see people scuba diving, relaxing on the small beach, and enjoying the views from the white granite rocks and the benches along the path. Plan on spending from one to three hours at this site.

Minnewaska State Park,
2589 US-44,
Gardiner, NY 12525

GPS 41.735096, -74.239039

Mohonk Preserve Visitor Center

Mohonk Preserve Visitor Center,
3197 U.S Hwy 4455,
Gardiner, NY 12525
41.734830, -74.187017

Mohonk Mountain House Barn Museum

Mohonk Mountain House Barn Museum,
High Falls, NY 12440
GPS 41.770351, -74.154179

1889 Eli Van Leuven cabin

Restored 1889 Eli Van Leuven cabin at Trapps Mountain
Hamlet National Historic District on the Mohonk Preserve.

Sam's Point Area of Minnewaska State Park Preserve

As you leave Pine Bush on
Route 52 you pass through
Walker Valley and then climb
to the top of the mountain
ridge. At the top is Sam's
Point, the once home of *Arthur
Geoffrey* the actor and
comedian.

Just past Sam's Point on the downside of Route 52 heading toward
Ellenville you may be lucky enough to pass under a *hang-glider* as he
or she jumps off the cliff heading toward the meadows in the valley
below. *(Valley shown)*

Sam's Point Area of Minnewaska State Park Preserve,
400 Sams Point Road,
Cragsmoor, NY 12420
GPS 41.670651, -74.361382

Scenic Parks for you to Visit

This Hudson Valley / River park listing is from the *scenichudson.org website,* they have links to each on their site and you are encouraged to visit the site and click their links for more information.

Bob Shepard Highland Landing Park
Black Creek Preserve
Clausland Mountain Park
Drayton Grant Park at Burger Hill
Emeline Park
Esopus Meadows Preserve
Esplanade Park
Esty & Hellie Stowell Trailhead at Storm King Mountain
Falling Waters Preserve
Fishkill Ridge
Foundry Dock Park
Four-Mile Point Preserve
Franny Reese State Park
Habirshaw Park
Harrier Hill Park
High Banks Preserve
Hudson Highlands Gateway Park
Hudson Highlands Nature Museum
Hyde Park Trail River Overlook
Illinois Mountain
Kathryn W. Davis RiverWalk Center
Lighthouse Park
Madam Brett Park
Manitou Point Preserve
Mawignack Preserve
Mount Beacon Park
Olana Viewshed
Peach Hill Park
Poets' Walk Park
RamsHorn-Livingston Sanctuary
Roosevelt Farm Lane
Scenic Hudson Mine Dock Park
Scenic Hudson Park at Irvington
Scenic Hudson Park at Peekskill Landing
Scenic Hudson RiverWalk Park at Tarrytown

Scenic Hudson's Long Dock Park
Scenic Hudson's Long View Park
Shaupeneak Ridge
Sleightsburgh Park
Walkway Loop Trail
Walkway Over the Hudson
West Point Foundry Preserve
Van der Donck Park at Larkin Plaza

Chapter # 14 … Railroads & Rail Trails

The Hudson Valley does NOT have many railroads as most have over the decades become old or obsolete due to the need for transporting coal and cement has subsided. Therefore, the only tracks that still remain are along the river and are either long-distance freight or Amtrak Passenger tracks. The obsolete tracks have been ripped up for their iron and wood, and the track beds have now either been allowed to return to nature or have been converted to bike and hiking trails. In some areas there are limited track being used for tourism, but mostly for display of engines or cabooses. Here are a few of the remaining.

Catskill Mountain Railroad

{Photo from the catskillmountainrailroad.com website}

This fun railroad has a 150-year history that dates back to the days of the Erie Canal and the need for a reliable transportation system in the Catskill Mountains.

Normally I would not include a complete website routing but the history of this is so interesting that I recommend its reading at https://www.catskillmountainrailroad.com/about-2/history/#

The railroad has added and subtracted routes, other railroads, and such for decades and was the blunt of political nonsense at one time. It has had many names and many ups-and-downs as storms, finances, and such tried to tear it apart. Volunteers rebuilt the line and have maintained it in good condition for the last decade or so.

Today the railroad provides several types of theme tours that are fun for the entire family. See their website for dates, times, and cost information.

Catskill Mountain Railroad,
Westbrook Lane Station,
149 Aaron Court,
Kingston, NY 12401
GPS 41.935439, -74.015099

Ellenville Rail Trail

Ellenville, NY 12428
41.720496, -74.381450

Gravity Railroad Display

D&H Canal Museum

The museum has displays of the workings of the canal and the gravity railroad that was used as part of the canal operations. See the D&H Canal Museum for the Gravity Railroad Display.

Kingston Point Rail Trail

Kingston, NY 12401
41.924730, -73.963233

Maybrook Railroad Museum

{Picture is from the villageofmaybrook.com website}

The Maybrook Railroad Museum is located at the side entrance of the Village of Maybrook Government Center at 111 Schipps Lane.

Check their website for dates and opening times.

Wikipedia has a very good write-up of the history of the Maybrook Train Yards.

Maybrook Railroad Museum,
111 Schipps Lane,
Maybrook, NY 12543
GPS 41.490849, -74.209750

Maybrook Caboose

Sitting in a small park along side of the highway is a single New Haven Red Caboose, good for a picture or two. This is part of the Maybrook Line of the New York, New Haven, and Hartford Railroad. It ran from Derby Connecticut to Maybrook, but in 1969 was merged with the Penn Central.

Maybrook Caboose,
973 Homestead Ave,
Maybrook, NY 12543
GPS 41.499315, -74.207596

Napanoch Train Station and Museum

Permanent Closed and part of the NYSDOC Eastern Correctional Facility.

Napanoch Train Station and Museum,
Napanoch, NY 12458
GPS 41.739737, -74.365241

O&W Railroad Station

Ontario & Western Railroad

Buildings are in Middletown, and in Roscoe. Roscoe is only open on weekends; the Middletown building is now part of the NPS and is not open due to a fire that destroyed parts of it. It was a 1892-93 Richardsonian Romanesque style building and it was augmented in 1904 and again in 1920.

O & W Building - Middletown

7 Low Ave,

Middletown, NY 10940
41.451864, -74.413157

O & W Building - Roscoe

7 Railroad Ave
Roscoe, NY 12776
41.931793, -74.912944

Rail Trail Caboose

This caboose is open on the weekends and has some of the history of the Rail Trail available to the visitors, bikers, and hikers of the Rail Trail.

Highland, NY 12528
41.710581, -73.956681

Rest Plaus O&W Rail Trail

Ontario & Western Railroad

These are bridges that cross the stream and other that crosses the Rest Plaus Road. Trail is being created from the old railroad bed.

O&W Rail Trail Bridge over the road

Stone Ridge, NY 12484
41.819790, -74.162688

Kripplebush Creek Bridge

New York
41.816327, -74.172898

Rosendale Trestle

{Postcard scan by the Rosendale Library is Public Domain}

This 940-foot Trestle bridge connects the rails from New Paltz to Kingston. It is 150-feet above the Rondout Creek and NY-213. It also spans the Delaware and Hudson Canal. The trestle was constructed in the

1870s and it opened as the highest span bridge in the USA on April 6, 1872. In 1895 the King Bridge Company due to safety concerns reinforced it.

Rosendale Trestle,
Wallkill Valley Rail Trail,
Rosendale, NY 12472
GPS 41.843326, -74.088031

Shawangunk, Walden, and Wallkill Rail Trail

This is an outing for the outdoors types that hike, ride bike, or do horseback riding. The trails are the remains of the old railroad lines

 that once flourished in the area when farming was the number one profitable activity.

Over the decades from the 1950s the farmers grew old and their farms were converted to housing, religious retreats, stores, and other activities, and thus there became little need for the rails to remain. The abandoned rails were removed for their scrap iron value, and the rail beds have become safe pathways for hiking and riding. *(Photo is from Wikipedia, author Daniel Case, it is Public Domain)*

Trolley Museum of New York

You get to take a trolley ride out to *Kingston Point Park*, and you get to see trolley cars dating from 1960 back to the 1897 era. They are also slowly adding a '911' survival vehicle area for your viewing; and they have some model trains.

89 E Strand Street,
Kingston, NY 12401
41.920203, -73.979827

Wallkill Valley Rail Trail

Per Wikipedia

"The Wallkill Valley Rail Trail is a 23.7-mile (38.1 km) rail trail and linear park that runs along the former Wallkill Valley Railroad rail corridor in Ulster County, New York. It stretches from Gardiner through New Paltz, Rosendale, and Ulster to the Kingston city line. The trail is separated from the Walden–Wallkill Rail Trail by two state prisons in Shawangunk, though there have been plans to bypass these facilities, and to connect the Wallkill Valley Rail Trail with other regional rail trails."

Portions of the trails have been paved, some of it not.

Please clean up after yourself and your animals, and enjoy the peace and serenity of the outdoors in the Hudson River Valley.

Yorktown Heights Rail Trail

North County Trailway

Parking Lot.
Yorktown Heights, NY 10598
41.231304, -73.779062

Footpath crossing road from the parking lot to the path to the bridge
255-233 NY-118
Yorktown Heights, NY 10598
41.230142, -73.778110

New Croton Reservoir Bridge

New York
41.227003, -73.776924

Chapter # 15 ... RV Campgrounds

There are campgrounds with RV spaces and hookups. These are different from the tent only campgrounds that may have a store, shower, and some fire pits, in that there are facilities for dumping gray or black water; water and electric hookups, and ample space for various sized RVs to maneuver without destroying the RV or the environment. Note that there may be many more campgrounds on private property, in State and Federal owned parks, and in some of the tent campgrounds. *See Campgrounds.*

Black Bear Campground

Black Bear Campground
197 Wheeler Road,
Florida, NY 10921
41.322222, -74.373698

Croton Point Park

This park is on land that natives inhabited centuries ago, it is now a 508-acre riverfront park with a boat launch, campground, fishing, picnic areas, and a playground & Radio Controlled aircraft area.

Croton Point Park
1 Croton Point Ave,
Croton-On-Hudson, NY 10520
41.186855, -73.892263

Interlake RV Park

Campground is on the upper end of what may be considered the Hudson Valley.

Interlake RV Park
428 Lake Drive,
Rhinebeck, NY 12572
41.905534, -73.812366

New York City North / Newburgh KOA Holiday

119 Freetown Hwy
Wallkill, NY 12589
41.637840, -74.100894

Oakland Valley Campground

Oakland Valley Campground
399 Oakland Valley Road,
Cuddebackville, NY 12729
41.479347, -74.622180

Rondout Valley RV Campground

Rondout Valley RV Campground
105 Mettacahonts Road,

Accord, NY 12404
41.796793, -74.251818

So-Hi Campgrounds

So-Hi Campgrounds
425 Woodland Road,
Accord, NY 12404
41.873304, -74.220029

Sylvan Lake Beach Park Inc

Sylvan Lake Beach Park Inc
18 McDonnell's Lane,
Hopewell Junction, NY 12533
41.604516, -73.745403

Yogi Bear's Jellystone Park™ Camp-Resort at Lazy River

Yogi Bear's Jellystone Park™ Camp-Resort at Lazy River
50 Bevier Road,
Gardiner, NY 12525
41.681353, -74.165475

Chapter # 16 ... Skiing Areas

Although the Hudson Valley has decent mountain ranges, most of the mountain property is either state park or privately owned, and thus there is limited space for ski area development. Here is a listing of some of the more popular ski areas.

Belleayre Mountain Ski Center

55 ski & snowboard trails, 8 lifts

Belleayre Mountain Ski Center
181 Galli Curci Road,
Highmount, NY 12441
42.132262, -74.505332

Catamount Mountain Resort

7 lifts, lessons & 3 terrain parks

Catamount Mountain Resort
78 Catamount Road,
Hillsdale, NY 12529
42.169140, -73.476935

Holiday Mountain Ski & Fun

Skip slope in winter, fun park in summer

Holiday Mountain Ski & Fun
99 Holiday Mountain Road,
Monticello, NY 12701
41.629600, -74.614492

Hunter Mountain

Mountain resort with simple condos

Hunter Mountain
64 Klein Ave,
Hunter, NY 12442
42.207772, -74.207797

Mount Peter Ski Area

Skiing, snowboarding & lessons
Mount Peter Ski Area
51 Old Mt Peter Road,
Warwick, NY 10990
41.247813, -74.295193

Mountain Trails Cross Country

Mountain Trails Cross Country
6198 Main Street,
Tannersville, NY 12485
42.195413, -74.142560

Old Silver Mine

Old Silver Mine Ski Center,
Stony Point, NY 10980
41.295601, -74.059387

Thunder Ridge Ski Area

Ski resort

Thunder Ridge Ski Area
2319, 137 Birch Hill Road,
Patterson, NY 12563
41.507940, -73.586090

Victor Constant Ski Area at West Point

Ski resort · West Point

West Point Golf Course
718 Victor Constant Road,
West Point, NY 10996
41.397395, -73.984004

Windham Mountain Resort

1,600 vertical ft. of skiing & 12 lifts

19 Resort Drive,
Windham, NY 12496
42.299144, -74.256048

Chapter # 17 ... Tours/Fairs & Fun Things to Do

The Hudson Valley is suited for camping, RV camping, boating, fishing, hunting, swimming, tubing, skiing, wire tasting, visiting historic museums and buildings, hiking, sightseeing, mountain climbing, hang gliding, and are mostly for outdoor activities year round. It is only miles from NYC, NJ, PA, CT, and VT. You will find that this listing of 'Things to Do' {Other than above} are mostly outdoor activities.

You need to visit towns like Pine Bush and those along the Shawangunk Mountains for information on Clambakes, Chicken Fries, Beer Fest, county fairs, fireworks, and much more as these activities are abundant in the warmth of the late spring, summer, and fall months.

Bear Mountain Ice Rink

Seven Lakes Drive,
Tomkins Cove, NY 10986
41.311374, -73.991257

Great Jack O'Lantern Blaze

The Blaze

This is a lighting show put on each year at Halloween at the Van Cortlandt Manor. Some 7,000 or so illuminated hand-carved pumpkins are on display at the estate.

Van Cortlandt Manor
525 S Riverside Ave,
Croton-On-Hudson, NY 10520
41.191658, -73.876509

Headless Horseman Hayrides and Haunted Houses

778 Broadway, Rte 9W,
Ulster Park, NY 12487
41.851737, -73.969193

Hudson River Adventures Pride of the Hudson

Hudson River Adventures Pride of The Hudson
90 Front Street,
Newburgh, NY 12550
GPS 41.503954, -74.004543

Hunter Mountain

64 Klein Ave,
Hunter, NY 12442
42.207783, -74.207807

Ahimsa Yoga & Music Festival

64 Klein Ave,
Hunter, NY 12442
42.204419, -74.210510

NYC Snow Bus - Ski & Snowboard Trips

64 Klein Ave,
Hunter, NY 12442
42.204477, -74.210435

Taste of Country Music Festival

64 Klein Ave,
Lanesville, NY 12450
42.204514, -74.211033

New York Zipline Adventures LLC

64 Klein Ave,
Lanesville, NY 12450
42.204514, -74.211033

Muscoot Farm Farmers Market

51 NY-100, Katonah, NY 10536
41.261259, -73.725004

New York Renaissance Faire

New York Renaissance Faire
600 NY-17A,
Tuxedo Park, NY 10987
41.249357, -74.226903

Skáldvik Viking Village at the New York Renaissance Faire

600 NY-17A,
Tuxedo Park, NY 10987
41.249364, -74.232526

Ridgeview Horse Stables & Riding Lessons

85 Hasbrouck Road,
New Paltz, NY 12561
41.731282, -74.171638

Skydive the Ranch

There is nothing like jumping out of a perfectly good aircraft to get the blood flowing. Have Fun!

55 Sand Hill Road,

Gardiner, NY 12525
41.674260, -74.150205

The Castle Fun Center

109 Brookside Ave,
Chester, NY 10918
41.361066, -74.286529

Chapter # 18 ... Wineries

Napa Valley of the East

Wineries in the Hudson Valley

The lower Hudson Valley for decades was home of Apple Orchards, Dairy Farms, and small Truck Farms.

The area in the late 1950s and beyond started to die off as the aging apple trees stopped producing, the corporations took over the dairy farms, and religions moved in and eliminated the truck farms (Farms that raised vegetables for market).

Shown is the Sugarloaf Winery.

The Valley became a residential area for the workers of New York City as plots of land disappeared into housing developments. The Pine Bush area was hard hit due to the new Route 17 being build and, thus bypassing the older Route 52 to the Catskills. This destroyed the resorts and the touring business that had survived for generations.

There was only one winery, the *Brotherhood Winery* that for years had been making some of the most delicious wines in the nation. It took the destruction of the area and its economy to wake people up; they finally decided to try their hand at growing wine grapes. And guess what, it worked; the area is now rich in wine grapes that have replaced the apples and small farm vegetable production. The lower

Hudson Valley is now the *Napa Valley of the east.* Here is a listing of some of the wineries you might put on your *'Wine Tour to Visit List'*.

Angry Orchard
Angry Orchard, 2241 Albany Post Road, Walden, NY 12586 - GPS 41.587349, -74.221747

Applewood Winery
Applewood Winery, 82 4 Corners Road, Warwick, NY 10990 - GPS 41.294650, -74.309879

Baldwin Vineyards
Baldwin Vineyards, 176 Hardenburgh Road, Pine Bush, NY 12566 - GPS 41.623086, -74.293948

Bashakill Vineyards
Bashakill Vineyards, 1131 S Road, Wurtsboro, NY 12790 - GPS 41.515068, -74.535617

Benmarl Winery
Benmarl Winery, 156 Highland Ave, Marlboro, NY 12542 - GPS 41.592862, -73.982203

Brimstone Hill Vineyard
Brimstone Hill Vineyard, 61 Brimstone Hill Road, Pine Bush, NY 12566 - GPS 41.627429, -74.315515

Brotherhood Winery

This is claimed to be the oldest winery in the United States.

From the brotherhood-winery.com website.

"Experience the enigmatic atmosphere of Brotherhood Winery by taking a leisurely stroll through our vast network of underground cellars. Excavated by hand in the late 19th Century, the dimly lit cellars house over two hundred oak barrels and feature a crested vault containing some of the oldest vintages in America.

Our team of knowledgeable guides will reveal the secrets of these mysterious vaults and keep you amused with tall tales of folly and tragedy. The tour will get you well acquainted with the complete wine making process and you will feel like an expert in the field."

They make a *holiday spiced wine* that is drank heated so that the mellowness of the spices present a bouquet to your nose and palate I still have an unopened 30-year old bottle that I kept as a keepsake; the other 11 bottles have been long gone.

Love the cellars, but the stairs are a climb after an hour of wine tasting and joviality with the tour presenters, especially if you are 'assisting' another that had a 'tad' too much.

Brotherhood Winery,
100 Brotherhood Plaza Drive,
Washingtonville, NY 10992
GPS 41.432445, -74.162990

Christopher Jacobs Winery at Pennings Vineyards
(Seasonally Open May-Oct)
Christopher Jacobs Winery at Pennings Vineyards, 320 Crawford St, Pine Bush, NY 12566 - GPS 41.586054, -74.363121

Clearview Vineyard
35 Clearview Lane, Warwick, NY 10990
41.301350, -74.348359

Demarest Hill Winery
81 Pine Island Turnpike
Warwick, NY 10990
41.263621, -74.374072

El Paso Winery Inc
El Paso Winery Inc, 742 Broadway, Ulster Park, NY 12487 - GPS 41.857144, -73.970540

Glorie Farm Winery
Glorie Farm Winery, 40 Mountain Road, Marlboro, NY 12542 - GPS 41.617810, -74.012620

Kettleborough Cider House
Kettleborough Cider House, 277 NY-208, New Paltz, NY 12561 - GPS 41.715674, -74.111584

Magnanini Winery, Restaurant & Distillery
Magnanini Winery, Restaurant & Distillery, 172 Strawridge Road, Wallkill, NY 12589 - GPS 41.597371, -74.152244

Millbrook Vineyards & Winery
Millbrook Vineyards & Winery, 26 Wing Road, Millbrook, NY 12545 - GPS 41.839885, -73.684649

Orange County Distillery
19 Maloney Lane
Goshen, NY 10924
41.352678, -74.390070

Palaia Winery
Palaia Winery, 10 Sweet Clover Road, Highland Mills, NY 10930 - GPS 41.379280, -74.099912

Robibero Winery
Robibero Winery, 714 Albany Post Road, New Paltz, NY 12561 - GPS 41.715006, -74.160988

Stoutridge Vineyard
Stoutridge Vineyard, 10 Ann Kaley Lane, Marlboro, NY 12542 - GPS 41.614066, -73.982355

The Kedem Winery
The Kedem Winery, 1519 US-9W, Marlboro, NY 12542 - GPS 41.623946, -73.965392

Torne Valley Vineyard
Torne Valley Road & Torne Brook Road, Hillburn, NY 10931
41.140332, -74.163431

Warwick Valley Winery & Distillery
114 Little York Road, Warwick, NY 10990
41.293493, -74.437745

Weed Orchards & Winery
Weed Orchards & Winery, 43 Mt Zion Rd, Marlboro, NY 12542 - GPS
41.623155, -74.000919

Whitecliff Vineyard & Winery
Whitecliff Vineyard & Winery, 331 Mckinstry Road, Gardiner, NY
12525 - GPS 41.686780, -74.201320

Wine Tour – Pine Bush Area – NY-17 to NY-17

From NY-17 Exit 119 take NY-302 east to County # 48 at Thompson
Ridge and go northwest to Crawford Street north and the *Christopher
Jacobs Winery at Pennings*. Stay on Crawford Street north to
Burlingham Road east to NY-52 and go south toward Pine Bush.
Turn left onto Bruynswick-New Prospect Road and then on
Brimstone Hill Road to the *Brimstone Hill Vineyards*. Backtrack to
NY-52 and go Pine Bush.

At the top of the bridge turn left onto Maple Avenue and follow it to
Hardenburg Road that will take you to the *Baldwin Vineyards*. Follow
Hardenburg Road to the Bruyn Turnpike and turn left; proceed to
the Bruynswick-New Prospect Road and turn right. At Dwaarkill
cross the bridge and turn left and follow county #7, Bruynswick
Road to County #7A Mckinstry Road and go east to the *Whitecliff
Vineyard & Winery*. Stay on #7A and then turn left onto County # 9
north to US-44. Turn right and go east on US-44 past the *Hudson
Valley Wine Market* to NY-32 at Modena. Turn left heading north to
Allhusen Road and then right to the *Adair Vineyards*. Backtrack to
NY-32 south and turn left heading west on US-44.

Go left at NY-208 south to County # 300 and go east to Plains Road
south. Turn left onto Strawridge Road and proceed to the *Magnanini
Winery, Restaurant & Distillery*. Take Strawridge (Borden's Road) west
to Wallkill and then cross the river onto Bruyn Turnpike and then left
on Albany Post Road south. Follow this to *Angry Orchard Cider
Brewing*. Take NY-208 at Walden and then to Washingtonville and

the *Brotherhood Winery*. NY-208 will then take you to NY-17 (US-6) at Exit 130.

Chapter # 19 ... Waterfalls

The Hudson Valley has many streams, creeks that flow to the Hudson River and eventually to the Atlantic Ocean at the New York Harbor. These streams and rivers start in the mountain areas and in some places create beautiful waterfalls. Note though that during the late hot summers and fall and winter months many of the streams do dry up; thus the best time to visit the waterfalls is just after the spring thaw or in the early summer months.

High Falls Historic Site

This is off of NY-213. High Falls was by the early settlers called the *'Great Falls'* and the area began to be settled in 1676.

Jacob Hasbrouck was one of the first residents of the area, and he built a stone house near the falls on the Rondout (Creek) River.

Several mills were built in the area to harness the power of the creek, and eventually a hydroelectric power plant was built and supplied the area with electric. In 1828 there was the discovery of hydraulic cement while the D&C canal was built.

Today all that remains is an old foundation, and the above sign to mark the location. If the nearby town there the canal locks, museum, and hiking trail that explains the history of the area.

Unnamed Road
High Falls, NY 12440
41.829182, -74.132397

High Falls - Great Falls

Marbletown
New York
116

41.830052, -74.132286

Ice Caves and Verkeerderkill Falls Trail Hike

It was once said that *Arthur Geoffrey* lived in the Sam's Point / Ice Caves area. (Author cannot verify this in September 2018),

Ice Caves and Verkeerderkill Falls Trail Hike,
Cragsmoor, NY 12420
GPS 41.674117, -74.352996

Indian Brook Waterfalls

Philipstown, NY
41.404973, -73.929164

Kaaterskill Falls

Famous tiered waterfall with a lookout

Kaaterskill Falls Viewing Platform
Laurel House Road,
Palenville, NY 12463
42.193849, -74.063624

Rainbow Waterfall

Ulster County
New York
41.714410, -74.276692

Stony Kill Falls

Short hikes to a cascading waterfall
Stony Kill Falls
Wawarsing, NY 12446
41.727603, -74.301542

Verkeerder Kill Falls

As a young boy this author and his friends would hike to these falls that were at the time unknown to most of the area's residents and visitors. We would 'skinny-dip' in the pool below the falls; catch fish and dig up the roots of the local water lilies and boil each like a potato. We picked wild black cherries from a tree nearby in addition

117

to elderberries, wild strawberries, walnuts, and various wild onions and thus, we had great all-day fun and healthy food. It was good times.

Verkeerder Kill Falls
Pine Bush, NY 12566
41.685247, -74.328001

Wallkill River Falls - Power Plant

Wallkill River - High Falls
Walden, New York
41.559814, -74.194594

Zabriskie's Waterfall

Annandale-On-Hudson, NY 12504
42.016920, -73.913577

Chapter # 20 … Zoos & Animal Parks

The Hudson Valley area is rich in animal life and in many areas you can see skunks, deer, rabbits, squirrels, frogs, chipmunks, pheasants, groundhogs, ducks, turkeys, snakes, foxes, mountain lions, and bears. The shame is that man is slowly taking the land from these creatures and many have had to adapt or perish.

The state allows hunting of most of the above animals and the state has not bothered to create many 'off-limits' areas or zoos. The following is what remains and it is a shame that one of the two has forever closed.

The Old Game Farm (Catskill Game Farm)

Closed in 2006, may reopen as a RV camp site in 2019)

From the *TheOldGameFarm.com* website

> *"The Catskill Game Farm closed in 2006 – it was the first privately owned zoo in the United States, operational from 1933-2006 and housed over 2,000 animals. Among their collection included Giraffes, Rhinos, Pygmy Hippos, Capybaras and many more. The zoo itself is approximately 150 acres with 3.5 miles of paved walkways and 130 structures. It is now often visited by people for the sake of nostalgia, urban exploration and/or photography."*

Advanced reservations are a must to see and walk the site. There is no charge to do so, but donations for keeping the site free and safe are recommended.

The author and his family are sad that an era came to an end; we had visited the Game Farm on several occasions and always enjoyed the hospitality and selection of animals.

Go to their website to see their future plans for the site.

The Old Game Farm, 400 Game Farm Road, Catskill, NY 12414 - GPS
42.235827, -74.007941

Trailside Museums & Zoo

This zoo takes in wild animals and attempts to 'fix' their injuries and
ailments. Most of the animals are from the Hudson Valley and
would not survive if not for the Trailside Zoo and its keepers.

There are trails that provide great views of the Hudson River, and
there are four museums that were built in the 1920s. The 1927
Herpetology house provides a look at all sorts of various snakes,
turtles, newts, frogs, toads, salamanders and much more.

The Nature Study Museum provides a look at various mammals and
the ways to identify each.

The Geology Museum provides a study of the rocks, earth, and
mineral formations in the Hudson Valley and how many of each was
commercially utilized.

The History Museum takes the viewer back to the days when Native
Americans and then European settlers called the valley their home.
The museum also features *Mr. Daniel Carter Beard* (1850-1941) the
illustrator for Mark Twain and Ernest Crosby.

In 1905 Mr. Beard founded the Sons of Daniel Boone organization
and then in 1910 the Boy Scouts of America. Plan on most of the day.

Trailside Museums & Zoo,
Tomkins Cove, NY 10986
GPS 41.317893, -73.989013

Appendix I - County City/Town Listing

Use this listing to determine the sites to see in each county. The
towns in which the sites are located are provided. If you do an e-
book search on a town name, you should be able to see a listing of all
the sites to visit in that town.

Columbia County

Hudson

Kinderhook

Dutchess

Annandale-On-Hudson
Beacon
Poughkeepsie
Red Hook
Staatsburg

Greene County

Catskill

Montgomery County

Amsterdam
Fort Hunter
Fort Johnson

Orange County

Bear Mountain
Campbell Hall
Cornwall-On-Hudson
Cuddebackville
Fort Montgomery
Goshen
Maybrook
Middletown
Monroe
Montgomery
New Windsor
Newburgh
Rock Tavern
Walden
Washingtonville

Putnam County

Cold Spring
Garrison

Rockland County

Haverstraw
New City
Nyack
Stony Point

Tomkins Cove
West Nyack

Sullivan County

Hurleyville
Wurtsboro

Ulster County

Cragsmoor
Ellenville
Gardiner
Kingston
Napanoch
New Paltz
Pine Bush
Rosendale
Saugerties
Wallkill

Westchester County

Buchanan
Cortlandt
Croton-On-Hudson
Irvington
Peekskill
Rye
Sleepy Hollow
Staatsburgh
Tarrytown
Yonkers

Index

Hudson Valley & Vicinity Attractions..1

Preface 1

Table of Contents..2

  Using this Touring Manual:...2

Chapter # 01 … Attractions 3

  5 Locks Walk...3

    Delaware and Hudson Canal from Locks 16 to 20 3

    D&H Canal Historical Society 3

    Rosendale Hydraulic Cement 3

  Albert K. Smiley Memorial Tower (Skytop Tower) 4

  Boscobel House and Gardens..5

  Carrollcliff 6

    Axe Castle 6

    Equus Restaurant...6

  Catskill Mountains...6

    Borscht Belt 6

    Shawangunk Mountains...6

  Catskills Visitor Center...7

  Cedar Grove..7

  Colden Mansion Ruins 7

  Constitution Marsh Audubon Center and Sanctuary..7

    Boardwalk Area 8

    Parking Area..8

  Decker House, Hoot Owl, Brett's, and the 1776 Inn 8

  Delaware and Hudson (D&H) Canal...9

    Gravity Railroads..9

    D&H Canal, ...9

    D&H Canal Museum...9

    D & H Canal Park 10

    Depuy Canal House 10

  Deyo Hall..10

  Dia:Beacon...10

  Discovery of Cement Marker 10

    Brooklyn Bridge and the Statue of Liberty 10

  Eleanor Roosevelt Center-Val-Kill..11

  Ever Rest..11

    Newington Cropsey Foundation...11

  Furgary Fishing Village...11

Shacks', the 'Shantytown', 'North Dock Tin Boat Association'
....11
Glynwood (Org) Farm...12
    Regenerative Agriculture 12
Gomez Mill House 13
Harden House...14
    Union Free School District of Tarrytown 14
    Old Croton Aqueduct Trail 14
Hudson River Sloop Clearwater..14
    Great Hudson River Revival 14
    Clearwater Festival..14
Hudson Valley Center for Contemporary Art.........................15
    Hudson Valley MOCA...15
Hudson Valley Old Time Power..15
Indian Point Energy Center 15
Jacob T Walden House (Old Hearthstone) 16
    'Kidd Town' 16
Jay Heritage Center...17
    1838 Peter Augustus Jay Mansion...17
    1907 Van Norden Carriage House 17
Karpeles Manuscript Library 18
King Mansion...18
    Tarrytown House Estate 18
Kykuit, the Rockefeller Estate 18
Lasdon Park, Arboretum & Veterans Memorial 19
Locust Grove Estate 19
Locust Lawn Estate..20
    Colonel Josiah Hasbrouck Estate...20
    Evert Terwilliger House...20
Lyndhurst Mansion 20
Manitoga / The Russel Wright Design Center 20
    Place of Great Spirit..20
Motorcyclepedia Museum 21
Newburgh Brewing Company...21
Newburgh Pier 21
Northgate, Cornish Estate...22
    Cornish Estate Trail Head 22
    Cornish Estate ruins 22
Old Rhinebeck Aerodrome..22
Onderdonck Tallman Budke House..23
    Jersey Dutch Stone House 23

Philipsburg Manor 23
Philipse Manor Hall State Historic Site 23
Rosen House 24
Scenic Hudson RiverWalk Park at Tarrytown 24
Sculpture of Headless Horseman 24
 Legend of Sleepy Hollow 24
Seven Lakes Drive 25
Shawangunk Ridge National Scenic Byway 25
Springwood 26
 President Roosevelt's Childhood Home 26
 President Roosevelt's Burial Place 26
Staatsburgh 26
 Tales of the Titanic 26
Stone Barns Center for Food and Agriculture 27
Stonecrop Gardens 27
Storm King Art Center 28
Sunnyside 28
Taconic Outdoor Education Center 28
Tarrytown Music Hall 28
The Palisades Parkway Visitor Center and Bookstore 29
The Temple of Virtue 29
 New Windsor Cantonment 29
Tillson Lake 29
 Palmaghatt Kill 29
Top Cottage (FDR's Retreat) 30
Tuthilltown Grist Mill 30
Union Church of Pocantico Hills 31
Van Cortlandt Manor 31
 The Manor of Cortlandt 31
Vanderbilt Mansion 31
Villa Lewaro 32
 Madam C. J. Walker 32
Washington Irving's Sunnyside 32
Widow Jane Mine 33
 Snyder Estate, Century House Historical Society 33
 Snyder Estate Natural Cement Historic District 33
Wilderstein 34
 Wild Man's Stone 34
Woodstock Farm Sanctuary 34
Chapter # 02 ... Beaches 35
 Bar Beach 35

Bear Mountain Park & Beach 35
Kingston Point Beach...36
Lake MacGregor Beach...36
Lake Tiorati Beach...36
Lake Welch Beach 36
Minnewaska Lake Beach...36
Nyack Beach State Park...37
Saugerties Village Beach 37
Sylvan Lake Beach Park Inc 37
Chapter # 03 ... Bridges...37
Bear Mountain – Purple Heart Bridge 37
Castleton-on-Hudson Bridge..38
Congress Street Bridge 38
Kingston-Rhinecliff Bridge 38
Newburgh-Beacon Bridge...38
Perrine's Covered Wallkill River Bridge..38
Poughkeepsie Bridge 38
Purple Heart Memorial Bridge...39
Rip Van Winkle Bridge..39
Tappan Zee Bridge...39
    Governor Malcolm Wilson Tappan Zee Bridge 39
    Governor Mario Cuomo Tappan Zee Bridge 39
Chapter # 04 ... Campgrounds...39
Agatha A. Durland Scout Reservation..40
Beaver Pond Campground 40
California Hill State Forest..40
Camp Bullowa 40
Camp Combe YMCA..40
Camp Floradan...41
Camp Hillcroft..41
Camp Lakota Sleepaway & Summer Camp Upstate NY 41
Camp Nabby..41
Camp Olmsted..41
Camp Redwood...41
Camp Yachad...42
Canopus Beach Complex 42
Challenge Camp..42
Clarence Fahnestock State Park..42
Durland Scout Reservation...42
Eden Village Camp 42
Fahnestock State Park Campground 43

Green Chimneys Summer Camp - Hillside.................................43
Group Sites 1 & 2...43
Henry Kaufman Camp..43
John V Mara Valley Camp...43
Kiwi Country Day Camp...43
Malouf's Mountain Campground......................................43
Marist Brothers Center at Esopus..................................44
Putnam Valley Parks and Recreation................................44
Rock Hill Camp..44
Rosmarin Day Camp...44
Sam Pryor Shawangunk Gateway Campground...........................44
Surprise Lake Camp..44
Sylvan Lake Beach Park Inc..45
Wayfinder Experience Inc..45
Wild Earth..45
YMCA Camp Wiltmeet..45
Chapter # 05 ... Climbing Areas...................................45
Bonticou Crag...45
Gunks at the Mohonk Preserve......................................46
The Trapps and the Lost City......................................46
Peter's Kill Area...46
Ramapo Powerlinez...46
Trapps Cliffs...46
Wallkill Valley Overlook - Gertrude's Nose........................47
Gertie's Nose...47
Chapter # 06 ... Graves & Burial Plots............................47
Andrew Carnegie Grave...47
Samuel Gompers Grave..48
American Federation of Labor......................................48
Cigar-Makers Union..48
Washington Irving Grave...48
William Rockefeller Mausoleum.....................................48
Chapter # 07 ... Hiking Trails....................................49
1777 Trail..49
Anthony Wayne Loop Trailhead......................................49
Anthony's Nose Trail Head...49
Appalachian Trail...50
Appalachian Trail Genesis...50
Appalachian Trail NJ-NY Border....................................50
Appalachian Trail Parking/ Tiorati Circle.........................50
Cat Rocks...50

    Fingerboard Shelter 50
    Fitzgerald Falls 50
    Wildcat Shelter 50
  Anthony Wayne Loop Trailhead 50
  Arden Surebridge Trail (red markers) 51
  Bear Mountain–Harriman State Park............................51
    Bear Mountain Doodletown Circuit 51
    Bear Mountain Hike Trail.......................................51
  Blue Mountain Reservation Loop 51
  Blue Mountain Trail..51
  Blue Trail – New Paltz..51
  Boston Mine Trail..51
  Boundary Trail...51
  Breakneck Ridge Bypass Trail 51
  Breakneck Ridge Trail 52
  Brook Trail..52
  Castle Point Trail 52
  Colden Trail 52
  Constitution Marsh Trail..52
  Cornell Mine Trail Head 52
  Cornish Trail 52
  Coxing Trail 52
  Croton Reservoir Walking Trail 52
  Dawn Trail..53
  Doodletown Trail Head 53
  DP(R) Trail Access 53
  Escarpment Trail 53
  Fanny Reese State Park Trails......................................53
  Gertrude's Nose / Minnewaska Trail 53
  Goethals Trail – West Point 53
  Green Trail – Ulster Park..53
  Hamilton Point Trail 53
  Hickory Hollow Road/Trail..54
  High Point Carriageway 54
  Horse Trail Yellow 54
  Howell Trail 54
  Hunter Brook/Ox Hollow Trail....................................54
  Indian Head Mountain Loop..54
  Japan Trailhead..54
  Jeep Trail..54
  Kingston Point Rotary Park Trails...............................54

Ladentown Mountain Trail 55
Long Path (aqua markers)...55
Lower Awosting Carriageway Parking Lot 55
Major Welch Trail Head 55
Millbrook Mountain Path 55
Millbrook Mountain Trail 55
Minnewaska Lake Trail Head 55
Minnewaska State Park Preserve.....................................55
Mohonk Hiking Parking Lot 56
Mohonk Preserve Spring Farm Trailhead Parking 56
Mohonk Preserve West Trapps Trailhead Parking Area 56
Moneyhole Mt. Trail 56
Mossy Brook Trail 56
Muskrat Trail 56
N County Trailway 57
North County Trail Park 57
N Lookout Trail 57
Notch Trail 57
Nurian Trail (White N markers) 57
O&W Trail Parking...57
Old Croton Aqueduct Trail...57
Old Ski Trail 57
Orange Trail – New Paltz..57
Panther Mt. Trail 58
Peekamoose-Table Trail Head..58
Pine Meadow Road/Trail 58
Pine Root Trail 58
Pipeline Trail..58
Plum Point Park Trails 58
Rainbow Falls Trail - Wallkill..58
Rainbow Falls Trail - Kerhonkson 58
RD Trail...59
Red Trail – New Paltz...59
Red Trail - Highland 59
Roosevelt Farm Lane Trail..59
Sams Point Fat/Foot, Road/Trail 59
Sawmill Trails 59
Scofield Lane Trail Orange 59
Shaupeneak Ridge Lower Parking Lot/White Trail...................59
Slide Fall 59
Slide Mountain Loop 60

Smiley Carriageway...60
Spring Farm Trailhead parking...60
Sterling Lake Loop 60
Sterling Ridge Trailhead 60
Stony Kill Carriageway (Abandoned)...................................60
Suffern - Bear Mountain Trail..60
Tanbark Trail, Phoenicia, NY 60
Timp Torne Trailhead..61
Trapps Trail - Undercliff Road 61
Undercliff Trail -Gardner 61
Undercliff Trail –Cold Spring..61
Upper Awosting Carriageway - Wallkill...............................61
Upper Awosting Carriageway - Gardiner.............................61
Verkeerderkill Falls Trail 61
Wallkill Valley Rail Trail 61
Washburn Trail..62
Wawarsing Turnpike Trail 62
White Bar trailhead 62
White Trail – New Paltz 62
White Trail - Highland 62
Yellow Trail – New Paltz 62
Yellow Trail - Highland..62
Chapter # 08 ... Historic Buildings/ Sites & Markers 62
Abigail Kirsch at Tappan Hill Mansion 63
    Hillcrest 63
    Tappan Hill Mansion 63
Clermont State Historic Site 64
Huguenot Street National Historic Landmark 64
    1799 House...65
    Bevier-Elting House (1698)..65
    Burying Ground 65
    Deyo House 65
    Die Pfalz 65
    Dubois House 65
    Freer House..65
    French Church 1717 65
    Hasbrouck House 66
    Jean Hasbrouck House..66
    New Paltz...66
    Stone Church 1773 66
    Walloon Church..66

Historic Huguenot Street..66
John Jay Homestead Historic Site.................................66
   Bedford House 66
Martin Van Buren National Historic Site 67
   Lindenwald..67
Montgomery Place Historic Estate 67
   Bard College - Montgomery Place Historic Estate....67
Mount Gulian Historic Site...68
Nevele Old Hotel Historical Landmark........................68
Olana State Historic Site..69
Perkins Memorial Tower...69
Staatsburgh State Historic Site 70
Thomas Cole National Historic Site 70
Thomas Jansen House 70
Torne Monument 71
   Popolopen Torne...71
Chapter # 09 ... Historical Societies.............................72
Century House Historical Society 72
   Widow Jane Mine 72
Friends of Historic Kingston 72
Historical Society Newburgh 72
Historical Society of Rockland County 73
Historical Society-Middletown 73
Chapter # 10 ... Lighthouses...73
Hudson Athens Lighthouse...73
Rondout Lighthouse 74
Saugerties Lighthouse 74
Sleepy Hollow Lighthouse...74
Stony Point Lighthouse 74
Lighthouse Park and Historical Marker 75
   Esopus Meadows Lighthouse 75
Chapter # 11 ... Military History Sites 75
Camp Shanks World War II Museum............................75
   Last Stop USA..75
   Shanks Village 75
Edmonston House...76
Fort Montgomery 77
Knox Headquarters...77
National Purple Heart Hall of Honor 78
New Windsor Cantonment State Historic Site 78
Washington's Headquarters State Historic Site...........78

West Point Military Academy 79
    Battle Monument 79
    Constitution Island 79
    Forts of West Point 80
    Fort Putnam...80
    West Point Academy..80
    West Point Foundry Preserve 80
    West Point Museum 81
    South Battery - West Point...81
Chapter # 12 ... Museums...81
  Brick House Historical Museum...81
  Bronck House Museum 82
    Pieter Bronck House 82
  D&H Canal Museum 82
  Edward Hopper House Museum & Study Center.....................82
  Fireman's Firefighting Museum...83
  Foundry School Museum...83
  Frances Lehman Loeb Art Center Museum 83
  Franklin D. Roosevelt Presidential Library and Museum 84
  Fred J. Johnston Museum..85
    Van Leuven Mansion 85
  Garrison Art Center Museum 85
  Harness Racing Museum & Hall 86
  Haverstraw Brick Museum Inc 87
  Hessel Museum of Art..87
  Hill-Hold Museum..88
  Hudson Highlands Nature Museum 88
    Outdoor Discovery Center 88
    Wildlife Education Center 88
  Hudson River Maritime Museum 88
  Hudson River Museum...89
    Glenview Historic Home Tour 89
    Nybelwyck Hall 89
  Katonah Museum of Art 90
  Klyne Esopus Museum...90
  Madam Brett Homestead Museum 90
  Montgomery Village Museum 91
    Wesley Hall..91
  Museum at Bethel Woods 91
    1969 Woodstock Festival...91
  Museum Village 92

Napanoch Train Station Museum...92
The Neversink Valley Museum of History and Innovation 92
    Lenape Native Americans 92
Orange County Farmers Museum...93
Orange County Firefighter Museum...93
Putnam History Museum 93
    Foundry School Museum 93
Quarryman's Museum 94
    Opus 40...94
Samuel Dorsky Museum of Art 94
Sullivan County Museum 94
Time and the Valleys Museum 95
    1930s Lost Catskill Farm 95
Van Wyck Homestead Museum 95
Velocipede Museum 95
Walter Elwood Museum 96
Chapter # 13 … Parks 96
Minnewaska State Park...96
Mohonk Preserve Visitor Center 97
    Mohonk Mountain House Barn Museum 97
    1889 Eli Van Leuven cabin..97
Sam's Point Area of Minnewaska State Park Preserve 97
Scenic Parks for you to Visit 98
Chapter # 14 … Railroads & Rail Trails 99
Catskill Mountain Railroad 99
Ellenville Rail Trail..100
Gravity Railroad Display 100
    D&H Canal Museum..100
Kingston Point Rail Trail...100
Maybrook Railroad Museum 100
    Maybrook Caboose...101
Napanoch Train Station and Museum 101
O&W Railroad Station...101
    Ontario & Western Railroad...101
    O & W Building - Middletown 101
    O & W Building - Roscoe 102
Rail Trail Caboose 102
Rest Plaus O&W Rail Trail..102
    Ontario & Western Railroad...102
    Kripplebush Creek Bridge 102
Rosendale Trestle 102

Shawangunk, Walden, and Wallkill Rail Trail 103
Trolley Museum of New York 103
Wallkill Valley Rail Trail..103
Yorktown Heights Rail Trail..104
    North County Trailway 104
    New Croton Reservoir Bridge...104
Chapter # 15 ... RV Campgrounds 104
Black Bear Campground 105
Croton Point Park...105
Interlake RV Park 105
New York City North / Newburgh KOA Holiday.....................105
Oakland Valley Campground 105
Rondout Valley RV Campground 105
So-Hi Campgrounds...106
Sylvan Lake Beach Park Inc..106
Yogi Bear's Jellystone Park™ Camp-Resort at Lazy River 106
Chapter # 16 ... Skiing Areas..106
Belleayre Mountain Ski Center 106
Catamount Mountain Resort...106
Holiday Mountain Ski & Fun 107
Hunter Mountain 107
Mount Peter Ski Area 107
Mountain Trails Cross Country 107
Old Silver Mine..107
Thunder Ridge Ski Area..108
Victor Constant Ski Area at West Point 108
Windham Mountain Resort...108
Chapter # 17 ... Tours/Fairs & Fun Things to Do........................108
Bear Mountain Ice Rink...109
Great Jack O'Lantern Blaze...109
    The Blaze 109
Headless Horseman Hayrides and Haunted Houses.................109
Hudson River Adventures Pride of the Hudson.........................109
Hunter Mountain 109
    Ahimsa Yoga & Music Festival..109
    NYC Snow Bus - Ski & Snowboard Trips 110
    Taste of Country Music Festival..110
    New York Zipline Adventures LLC..110
Muscoot Farm Farmers Market...110
New York Renaissance Faire 110

Skáldvik Viking Village at the New York Renaissance Faire
....110
   Ridgeview Horse Stables & Riding Lessons 110
   Skydive the Ranch...110
   The Castle Fun Center 111
Chapter # 18 ... Wineries 111
   Napa Valley of the East..111
   Wineries in the Hudson Valley...111
   Brotherhood Winery 112
   Wine Tour – Pine Bush Area – NY-17 to NY-17 115
Chapter # 19 ... Waterfalls 116
   High Falls Historic Site..116
   High Falls - Great Falls 116
   Ice Caves and Verkeerderkill Falls Trail Hike 117
   Indian Brook Waterfalls 117
   Kaaterskill Falls 117
   Rainbow Waterfall 117
   Stony Kill Falls..117
   Verkeerder Kill Falls 117
   Wallkill River Falls - Power Plant...118
   Zabriskie's Waterfall 118
Chapter # 20 ... Zoos & Animal Parks 119
   The Old Game Farm (Catskill Game Farm) 119
   Trailside Museums & Zoo 120
Appendix I - County City/Town Listing...120
   Columbia County 120
   Dutchess...121
   Greene County 121
   Montgomery County..121
   Orange County..121
   Putnam County 121
   Rockland County 121
   Sullivan County 122
   Ulster County 122
   Westchester County...122
Index..123
Author 135
Cover Picture..136

Author

William (Bill) C. McElroy lived in the Hudson Valley from 1944 to 1956, and again off an on in the 1959 to 1980 era. His parents lived there for decades until the 2010 period, and he and his parents frequently visited the various historic, natures, and other attractions. His knowledge of the area includes personal history of many of the attractions and how each has changed over the decades. As an example how *Gertie's Nose* was named, and how the name was eventually changed to the *Gunks*.

Bill originally (1944-1956) lived in a farmhouse that dated back to 1883 and had hand-hewn beams, saw-cut flooring with bark intact, field-stone fireplace and foundation, pot-belly stove, 12-foot deep hand-dug well, and several out buildings including a three hole outhouse (hey, we were rich, not). His father was in the US Army, his mother and he took care of two-dozen cows, several chickens, many pigs, a dog, and 33 cats. On occasion there were baby pigs, cows, and dozens of mice living within the confines of the home's kitchen. It was fun times.

The US Army in 1956 caused the move to Texas, and upon return the USAF caused Bill to venture out into the world at age 18. He has traveled and circumnavigated the globe and has toured the USA ever since. His knowledge of the New York area, the American West and Southwest is vast and is displayed in his series of Amazon Kindle e-books that include:

> 100+ Tucson and Vicinity Attractions
> Philadelphia and Vicinity Attractions
> California / Oregon / Nevada Loop
> Explore South Dakota's Many, Many Attractions

 RoadSites tm travel manuals on Arizona, Colorado, New Mexico, and Utah, 40-days to a Career as a Tour Guide and many more under the names of William C. McElroy and William (Bill) C. McElroy.

Cover Picture

Minnewaska State Park off of the *Shawangunk Ridge National Scenic Byway.*

I believe this is looking toward the beach and the Catskill mountains from the south side of the lake where you can view the Hudson Valley above New Paltz.
2010-02-22-1853-44.jpg

Printed by Amazon Italia Logistica S.r.l.
Torrazza Piemonte (TO), Italy

59960498R00077